DIVIDED DUTIES

CARE PLANNING FOR CHILDREN WITHIN THE FAMILY JUSTICE SYSTEM

DIVIDED DUTIES

CARE PLANNING FOR CHILDREN WITHIN THE FAMILY JUSTICE SYSTEM

Being: Papers given to the President's inter-disciplinary conference for judges, directors of social services, mental health professionals, academics, guardians ad litem, panel managers and other professionals, held at Highgate House, Northampton, between 14 and 16 September 1997, together with a record of the discussions which took place in the plenary sessions of the conference.

Edited by

THE RT HON LORD JUSTICE THORPE

and

ELIZABETH CLARKE

of Gray's Inn, Barrister, Queen Elizabeth Building, Temple

With a Foreword by

SIR STEPHEN BROWN

President of the Family Division

Family Law

1998

Published by
Family Law, a publishing imprint of
Jordan Publishing Limited
21 St Thomas Street
Bristol BS1 6JS

British Library Cataloguing-in-Publication Data
A catalogue record for this book is available from the British Library.

ISBN 0 85308 520 X

Phototypeset by Mendip Communications Ltd, Frome
Printed in Great Britain by Hobbs The Printers Ltd of Southampton

CONTRIBUTORS

The Hon Mr Justice Wall

Dr Claire Sturge, Consultant Child Psychiatrist, Northwick Park Hospital

Jenny Kenrick, Child Psychotherapist, Tavistock Clinic

Peter Kemp, Director of Social Services, Durham County Council

Steven Ford, Social Worker, Social Services Department, Durham County Council

Professor Olive Stevenson, Professor Emeritus of Social Work Studies, University of Nottingham

Arran Poyser, Social Services Inspector, Department of Health

Michael Leadbetter, Director of Social Services, Essex County Council

Tess Duncan, Guardian ad Litem and Panel Manager, Surrey County Council

Anne Chan, Assistant Director of Social Services, Southwark Council

Gloria McFarlane, Social Worker, Social Services Department, Southwark Council

Professor Judith Harwin, University of Sussex

FOREWORD

Highgate House Conference
14–16 September 1997

Inter-disciplinary Co-operation in every Department was the all-pervading theme of a memorable conference held last September at Highgate House in Northamptonshire.

Organised under the umbrella of the President of the Family Division's Inter-disciplinary Committee, a distinguished assembly of Judges, Directors of Social Services, Medical Consultants, Academics, members of Child Care Agencies and other professionals met to discuss and consider the planning, provision and maintenance of effective child care services.

Elizabeth Clarke, an enthusiastic rising member of the Family Bar, has edited and produced an excellent and comprehensive record of their endeavours.

I hope and believe that it will provide food for thought as well as encouragement to all who are engaged in this vitally important field.

SIR STEPHEN BROWN
PRESIDENT OF THE FAMILY DIVISION

CONTENTS

EDITOR'S INTRODUCTION

The Rt Hon Lord Justice Thorpe

If we were in the Hollywood business, this book would be called *Rooted Sorrows II* but that would prevent Margaret Wall from mining the rich seam of her Shakespearean scholarship and from providing us with another title which is both extraordinarily apt and immediately identifiable. To her, the editors and publishers are again deeply grateful.

If the full potential of the President's biennial Inter-disciplinary Conference is to be achieved, it is crucial that the papers and the discussion which they generate should be published. So *Divided Duties* is the second in a series initiated by *Rooted Sorrows* and to be continued in the millennium year with the publication of the 1999 conference, provisionally themed on the Family Law Act 1996. No apologies are required for such a predictable choice because no statutory implementation has ever presented interdisciplinarity within the family justice system with a greater challenge.

It is gratifying to report with a retrospective glance that *Rooted Sorrows* has, to date, sold over 1,500 copies and I am confident that *Divided Duties* will outstrip that total, if only because its path is smoothed by the renown of the first born and because it addresses a less theoretical theme. The sales figure is due in part to the commitment of the Department of Health who block purchased a significant number of copies as did the Judicial Studies Board to a lesser extent. Thanks for the success of *Rooted Sorrows* are also due to Richard Hudson of Jordans who took the risk of publishing in an untested market.

As you read on, you will find a brief note of what I said both in opening and in closing the 1997 conference. What that note cannot convey is the feelings of the participants either expressed or palpable at two moments separated only by 48 hours. I had not anticipated the concern, apprehension and opposition to the suggestion that the princial task of the conference should be to consider to what extent guardians and courts should be re-empowered after the making of a care order. But the work done by the delegates both in the scheduled sessions and informally after hours was striking for its commitment to understand the other disciplines' positions and to stifle proposals that would have little chance of general acceptance. That virtue carried to extreme might have resulted in insubstantial outcome and verbiage where specific proposals were needed. Perhaps I should not make choices where all contributed evenly, but the way was undoubtedly paved for us by the work that Arran Poyser had been doing in response to the consensus at the President's conference for the designated judges in May 1997. Then, both the mental health professionals and the guardians worked tirelessly and constructively amongst themselves after hours. Finally, Michael Leadbetter and Peter Kemp showed how confident professionals can receive criticism positively. By the closing session, as the results from the groups demonstrate, there was a broad consensus that the needs of children in care demand change to our present system in the final stages of preparation for trial, at the trial itself when the court and the local authority are at odds over the proposals of the care plan, and finally in the subsequent implementation of the care plan. Of course there were a number of different methods advanced for achieving change.

This broad consensus was reflected in a marked change of atmosphere at the closing session. There was an enthusiasm for what had been achieved and for carrying the conference proposals forward. This atmosphere was confirmed by the unusually full and enthusiastic letters that delegates subsequently wrote to express their gratitude for the experience of the conference. That gratitude is due equally to the Department of Health and the Judicial Studies Board who bore the cost of the conference.

As I write this introduction six months on, what progress is discernible? First, a spontaneous movement arose from the November meeting of the President's Inter-disciplinary Committee and a report of the work of those professionals from mental health, social work, and children's representation is included as the final chapter of *Divided Duties.* If I had to choose one chapter for a reader who did not have time for more, this would be it. It distills, with the aid of reflection and exchange, the conference contributions into specific proposals that deserve to be tested and that must not go unnoticed by those who have the power to introduce change.

Clearly, what *Divided Duties* has the power to influence is change in practice and procedure at stage one, preparation for trial. Changes at stages two and three, the trial and subsequent implementation, are more heavily dependent on legislation. In that regard, although legislative change is extraordinarily hard to influence, I am not without some optimism. Arran Poyser's paper illustrates that the Department of Health is open minded. As to the Lord Chancellor's Department, I take heart from Hansard of 11 December 1996 where in debate Lord Irvine said:

> 'Next, the Children Act. One problem I identify is its failure to trust the judges sufficiently . . . I understand that the court should not be an appeal tribunal on day to day decisions in relation to the care of the child, but the absolute refusal to permit the judge any say at all in the child's future may well be wrong. An incoming Government will wish to give serious consideration to, and consult on, restoring to our judges the ability to tailor court orders to meet the justice of the particular cases.'

Furthermore, once the European Convention of Human Rights is legislated, Article 6 rights may breach the wall that effectively prevents a return to the court once a care order has been made.

However, even if my optimism is unfounded, that does not signal a sterile result. Modest adjustments can be achieved by interdisciplinary co-operation and commitment to reduce the risk of drift or breakdown in the implementation of the care plan. You only have to reflect on how many of the innovations proposed in the group results would be achievable without primary legislation.

An inevitable limitation on the President's Interdisciplinary Conference is that to be manageable it must be confined to about sixty places and all who are invited must be representative of the highest level of expertise in their fields of work. It is for *Divided Duties* to disseminate the conclusions of the conference more widely, to enlarge consultation, and to stimulate debate. If it achieves that objective its editors, contributors, and publishers will be well pleased.

Speaking of editors obliges me to confess that I have been little more than a conduit. The real work throughout has been done by Elizabeth Clarke. She diligently noted all that passed at Highgate whilst remaining at all times a convivial and popular member of the conference. Since then she has amazed me with the speed and efficiency of her work. Of course, knowing that she had been proposed by Florence Baron, I should have expected no less.

My final and my most significant words must be of gratitude to the President who has been generous and unfailing in his support for interdisciplinarity and who chaired his conference sessions with his inimitable charm and affability guaranteed both to dispel suspicion, tension and rivalry and to draw from all their best contributions.

INTRODUCTORY REMARKS

In introducing the first plenary session, Lord Justice Thorpe suggested that a question for consideration over the course of the conference might be to produce a formulation for possible revision of the present statutory division of function between judiciary and social services. Questions to be considered in such a formulation might include:

(a) who should be able to bring proceedings back to court for review. Should it be limited to perhaps the guardian ad litem?;

(b) should there be a requirement of leave as a filter for such applications?; and

(c) could one define clear circumstances which would need to exist before review should be initiated?

FIRST SESSION

CARE PLANS: A JUDICIAL PERSPECTIVE

The Hon Mr Justice Wall

SUMMARY OF PAPER

Mr Justice Wall introduced his paper by saying that in his view there was a consensus amongst family judges that the working of the Children Act in relation to care proceedings was in some respects unsatisfactory. He emphasised that it was of course recognised that the formulation of care plans and their implementation after the making of an order were not easy but he nevertheless felt that there were situations where it was both contrary to the interests of the child and frustrating for the judge to have no further involvement in a particular case. There were cases which for one reason or another had gone badly wrong after the making of the care order. He suggested that the court could be a useful forum for trying to resolve difficulties arising in the implementation of the care plan. He also stressed the importance on a practical level of managerial input in the formulation of care plans, which ideally should make clear who is responsible for the plan and the decision-making process behind such plans (perhaps in an introductory paragraph similar to that in many experts' reports) so that the judge knew how the plan had been formulated.

INTRODUCTION

The care plan, from the judicial perspective, is a curious animal. It makes no appearance in the Children Act 1989 or in the Family Proceedings Rules 1991. It is not a statutory document.[1] Yet, in practice, it has become a document of critical importance in every care case.

In my view, the importance the court attaches to the care plan is directly related to the structure of Part IV of the Children Act, which (save in limited and strictly defined respects) renders both the court and the guardian ad litem *functus officio*[2] once a care order is made. Furthermore, since the court cannot impose conditions on a care order[3] and since the court is duty bound to treat the welfare of the child as its paramount consideration in deciding whether or not a care order should be made,[4] it is both inevitable and right that the court will wish to scrutinise the care plan in order to satisfy itself that what the local authority proposes for the child is appropriate and in the child's interests. The tensions which this process is capable of generating and has generated in some of the reported cases will be a major theme of this paper.

Practical issues

I have little to add to the advice contained in paragraph 2.62 of volume 3 of the Department of Health *Children Act 1989 Guidance and Regulations*[5] and, more particularly, in chapter 14 of the admirable book by Joyce Plotnikoff and Richard Woolfson *Reporting to Court under the Children Act*,[6] both of which – but particularly the latter – are, I hope, required reading in all social services

---

1 *Re L (Sexual Abuse: Standard of Proof)* [1996] 1 FLR 116 at 126 per Butler-Sloss LJ. It does, however, of course appear in the *Children Act 1989 Guidance and Regulations* Volume 3: Family Placements at para 2.62: see *Manchester City Council v F* [1993] 1 FLR 419, per Eastham J and *Re J (Minors) (Care: Care Plan)* [1994] 1 FLR 253 at 259; see also Appendix 1 to this paper, where *Re J* is reproduced. It was also pointed out by Iain Hamilton at the conference that the Arrangements for Placement of Children (General) Regulations 1991 impose a statutory duty on responsible authorities, so far as is reasonably practicable, to make immediate and long-term arrangements for the placement of children whom they are looking after and to record those arrangements in writing. He argued that these records of the arrangements made for the child are therefore statutory, and that a difference of terminology should not derogate from the proposition that the duty of local authorities to make plans for the care of children is a continuous process which begins at the earliest stages of their involvement with the individual child. Iain Hamilton's argument is set out in full at Appendix 2 to this paper.

2 ie having performed their function and to whom further resort is incompetent, their functions being exhausted.

3 *Re T (A Minor)(Care Order: Conditions)* [1994] 2 FLR 423, CA.

4 *Re J* (*supra*) [1994] 1 FLR 253 at 258, principle (3).

5 HMSO, 1991: ISBN 011 32175 1.

6 HMSO, 1966: ISBN 011 321 968 7.

departments and will go a long way to resolving the difficulties referred to by Dame Margaret Booth in her report *Avoiding Delay in Children Act Cases*.[1]

I shall learn at the conference whether or not I speak for the judiciary as a whole when I say that what I look for in a care plan is what Plotnikoff and Woolfson describe as 'clear objectives for the care of children and a strategy for their achievement'.[2] The contents of paragraph 2.62 of volume 3 of the *Guidance and Regulations* are a checklist, most of the items of which are likely to apply in most cases. But no judge, I think, requires a particular format: what matters is that the care plan should be carefully adapted to the needs of the particular child and cover fully how those needs will be addressed if a care order is made.

I particularly endorse three points which Plotnikoff and Woolfson make. The first is that the care plan should be based on a realistic allocation of resources. Increasingly in my experience the court needs to be satisfied that a care plan has been properly costed and is financially capable of being put into effect.

The second point is their statement that it may be appropriate for the care plan to be endorsed by the social services manager. Indeed, I would go further than this.

In her report,[3] Dame Margaret Booth deals with the subject of local authority decision making and comments that the judiciary and legal profession do not generally appear to understand it or regard it as important. She says they frequently assume that individual social workers have greater authority than in fact is the case. She comments that to avoid the difficulties and tensions that such misunderstandings can give rise to there appears to be a need for local authorities to make the process by which relevant decisions must be reached more generally known. She also reports the perception that social work evidence is undervalued in court, thereby giving rise to a strong sense of demoralisation amongst social workers and in social services departments.

These observations have a direct relevance to and connection with the care plan. The process by which the care plan comes into being, and the decision-making process surrounding it, are, in my experience, frequently obscure. Often, the author of the care plan, and the person who speaks to it in court, is the social worker who has had the day-to-day conduct of the case on the ground. That worker is often inexperienced. This has several unfortunate side effects. First, it overburdens the social worker. Secondly, it makes it difficult for the social worker to maintain a positive working relationship with the family. Thirdly, if the social worker is inexperienced, it takes him or her into areas of policy (and perhaps funding) which are not his/her province.

In an ideal world, I would like to see the social worker on the ground concentrating on and limiting him/herself to what I call, without detracting from its importance, the 'leg-work'; factual observation and comment on that observation; where appropriate social work assessment and reporting on the assessment. I would like to see the team leader or a social services manager take responsibility for the care plan, and to speak to it in court.

In my judgement, this process would resolve a number of the difficulties to which Dame Margaret refers, and it would help to give the care plan the status and importance it deserves. I appreciate that what I am proposing has resource implications, but I am in no doubt that it would save time, money and stress in court.

My third specific point of endorsement for Plotnikoff and Woolfson is that they repeat the advice of the Children Act Advisory Committee,[4] often overlooked, on advance planning for children who are to be put forward in the care plan for adoption. They say:

> 'Care plans should be as full as the facts of an individual case allow. For example, where a permanent substitute family is planned, it is helpful if a range of possible adopters are identified and there is no reason why the Adoption Panel should not have become involved so long as the child has not been directly involved eg in meetings or placement. The crucial distinction is between planning in advance of the court's decision (which is to be encouraged) and on the other hand pre-empting the decision of the court.... Local authorities should have these matters in mind when preparing the care plan in order to avoid unnecessary delays.'

1 July 1996.
2 So far as I am aware, no dissent was expressed to this proposition at the conference.
3 Para 3.33.
4 Report 1993/4, p 32.

The role of the court in the decision-making process under Part IV of the Act

My thinking on the subject of the division of responsibility between the courts and local authorities on the making and implementation of care orders is set out in *Re J (Minors) (Care Plan)*.[1] A copy of the report of *Re J* is attached to this paper as Appendix 1.

It remains my view that the courts respect the division of responsibility between the courts and local authorities which is addressed in *Re J* and *Re L*. The court has to tread a delicate path between the extremes of inappropriate interference with matters properly within the ambit of the local authority's responsibility and equally inappropriate passivity in the face of poor social work practice. The process can generate substantial tension, but it remains my opinion that none of the reported decisions which I shall discuss in this paper oversteps the mark.

The responsibility for making care orders

Much of what follows is again obvious and trite, but precisely because it is obvious it is in great danger of being disregarded.

The critical starting point for any discussion of care orders under Part IV of the Children Act 1989 is that Parliament has entrusted the discretion to make or to refuse to make a care order to judges and magistrates, and only to judges and magistrates. This is the critical difference between Part III and Part IV of the Act. Under Part III, with the sole exception of secure accommodation orders under section 25, Parliament has entrusted provision of services for children and their families exclusively to local authorities. The courts have recognised that this is the case, and that the only remedy open to an aggrieved child or parent is by way of judicial review.[2]

However, when it comes to care or supervision orders under Part IV the power to make such orders is given exclusively to the court. The criteria are stringent, commensurate with the seriousness of the orders being sought.[3] As the courts have made clear on many occasions, a care order which may remove a child from his natural family, gives parental responsibility to a public body and entitles that body to determine the extent to which a parent or guardian of the child may meet his parental responsibility for the child – in other words an order which is likely to determine the whole course of a child's life and may well result in the permanent exclusion of his parents from his life – could not be more fundamental.[4]

The decision under section 31 whether or not to place a child in care is a two-stage process. First, the threshold criteria – themselves stringent – have to be satisfied. Secondly, the court has to be satisfied that such an order is in the child's interests, taking his welfare as the paramount consideration.

Given the importance of the decision and the stringency of the criteria it is in my view inevitable that the court:

(a) requires the fullest possible information about the child; and
(b) requires to be satisfied that the local authority's care plan fully meets the needs of the child so far as it is practicable to do so.[5]

---

1 [1994] 1 FLR 253, approved by the Court of Appeal in *Re L (Sexual Abuse: Standard of Proof)* [1996] 1 FLR 116, CA. Between them, I venture to suggest that they reflect current judicial thinking on the subject of care plans.

2 See *Re T (Accommodation by Local Authority)* [1995] 1 FLR 159, in which Johnson J granted *certiorari* to quash the decision of a director of social services that T's welfare would not be seriously prejudiced if she were not provided with accommodation under section 21; followed by myself in *Re J (A Minor) (Specific Issue Order: Leave to apply)* [1995] 1 FLR 669 (the court has no power to declare by way of specific issue order that a particular child is a child in need under section 17 of the Act: Parliament has decreed that it is for local authorities to decide whether or not a child is in need under section 17(1) of the Act: the child's only remedy is by way of judicial review of the local authority's decision that he is not a child in need).

3 See the speech of Lord Nicholls of Birkenhead in the recent decision of the majority of the House of Lords in *Re H (Minors) (Sexual Abuse: Standard of Proof)* [1996] 2 WLR 8, [1996] 1 All ER 1, [1996] 1 FLR 80, HL.

4 The *locus classicus* for the expression of the seriousness of this course of action is, of course, the speech of Lord Templeman in *Re KD (A Minor)* [1988] AC 806, 812.

5 The fact that the court must appoint a guardian ad litem in specified proceedings is mandatory unless the court is satisfied that it is not necessary to do so in order to protect the interests of the child (Children Act 1989, section 41) emphasises the importance of the decision, as do the wide-ranging powers given to the guardian ad litem under the Family Proceedings Rules and section 42 of the Act – powers which have been upheld by the court – see *Manchester City Council v T* [1994] Fam 181.

However, at the point the decision is made, it is the responsibility of the judge and the judge alone to decide the child's future.

The tension between the care plan and the judge's perception of welfare

It is at this vital point of decision that the difficulties begin. What if the judge disagrees with the care plan and the local authority decline to alter it? For example, the judge may think that the child should live at home under a care order, because despite past or likely future damage from his parents, the child retains a bond with them which should not be broken but which also requires the local authority to share parental responsibility for the child together with social work protective measures and general oversight for the protection of the child. The local authority's plan is for the child to be placed for adoption. It refuses to budge. The court cannot make a care order with a condition that the child lives at home. In such a case the judge may be forced to choose between sending the child home without local authority protection or making a care order the result of which will be a placement which the judge does not think to be in the interests of the child. Both results are highly unsatisfactory, and not in the interests of the child in question. The judge's duty is to take the child's welfare as his paramount consideration, but because he cannot require the local authority to take a given course, and has no supervisory jurisdiction in relation to the child after a care order has been made, he cannot make the order which he perceives to be in the child's interests.[1]

In *Re S and D (Children: Powers of Court)*[2] the boot was on the other foot. The judge was horrified at the local authority's care plan that two children should be rehabilitated to their mother's care. He refused to make a care order, but instead purported to make an order restraining the mother from removing the children from the homes of their foster carers. That was an order which he plainly did not have jurisdiction to make.

Aptly summarising the dilemma faced by judges in this situation, Balcombe LJ said:[3]

> 'The judge is therefore faced with the dilemma with which this judge was faced that, if he makes a care order, the local authority may implement a care plan which he or she may take the view is not in the child or children's best interests. On the other hand, if he makes no order, he may be leaving the child in the care of an irresponsible and indeed wholly inappropriate parent.
>
> It seems to me that, regrettable though it may seem, the only course he may take is to choose what he considers to be the lesser of two evils. If he has no other route open to him – and certainly the route chosen by the judge in this case was one which, in my judgment was not open to him – then that is the unfortunate position he has to face.
>
> I have to say that this is not a position to which judges who exercise jurisdiction in the family courts are unaccustomed . . ..'

The most extreme and worrying example of this lack of judicial power is, of course, the *Nottinghamshire* case.[4] In that case, a local authority refused to take care proceedings even though it acknowledged that the father of the children in question was a sexual abuser with a repetitive cycle of offending over many years who presented an unacceptable risk to his children who were living under the same roof. The mother, who supported the father, also refused to apply for prohibited steps orders which would have excluded the father from the home.

The court thus found itself powerless to make any appropriate order designed to protect children from the father. The President's comment on the Act is worth repeating:[5]

> 'The court is deeply concerned at the absence of any power to direct this authority to take steps to protect the children. In the former wardship jurisdiction it might well have been able to do so. The operation of the Children Act 1989 is entirely dependent upon the full co-operation of all those involved. This includes the courts, local authorities, social workers, and

1 At the conference, Bracewell J produced a chilling example of this dilemma. A mother was serving a prison sentence for injuries to a child, and on release was likely to return to live with her own mother, the child's maternal grandmother. Psychiatric evidence called by the guardian ad litem was to the effect that the child would be in danger if living in the same household as the mother. Despite this, the local authority's care plan was for the child to live with the grandmother. Bracewell J's view was that such a course was dangerous for the child and contrary to her interests. She was of the opinion that the child should be adopted. However, since there was nobody else to care for the child, she was constrained to make a care order.

2 [1995] 2 FLR 456.

3 [1995] 2 FLR 456 at 464.

4 [1994] Fam 18, CA.

5 [1994] Fam 18 at 43.

> all who have to deal with children. Unfortunately, as appears from this case, if a local authority doggedly resists taking the steps which are appropriate to the case of children at risk of suffering significant harm it appears that the court is powerless. The authority may perhaps lay itself open to an application for judicial review but in a case such as this the question arises, at whose instance? The position is one which it is to be hoped will not recur....'

In *Re T (A Minor) (Care Order: Conditions)*[1] the Court of Appeal added by way of comment on the *Nottinghamshire* decision:

> 'We have no doubt that there are other circumstances in which the court's wish to impose a particular result which it perceives to be in the interests of the child will be frustrated by the restrictions on the court's powers imposed by Part IV.'

I would be reasonably confident that each of the judges reading this paper in advance of the conference could give examples from his or her own experience of the tension I am describing.[2] I will give just two more examples from my own experience, the first of which contains an unhappy variant based on the 'resources' issue.

I have now several times been faced with what I regard as the unattractive argument from a local authority which tells the court that if a care order is made it will make considerable resources available to implement the care plan, whereas if the court refuses to make a care order and imposes a result with which the local authority disagrees, no such resources will be made available to implement the court's order, even if, as is *ex hypothesi* the case, the order is one which the court perceives to be in the best interests of the child.

One recent experience of this phenomenon was in what I describe generically as 'an undamaged or surviving sibling case' where the choice was between placement of a two-year-old child with the man who, up until DNA tests ruled him out, thought he was the child's father and placement of the child with her maternal grandmother. The case was finely balanced: both placements were fraught with difficulty, and each cried out for a care order. But the local authority's final care plan was for placement with the father. It would not contemplate placement with the grandmother. Thus I could not place the child with the grandmother under a care order.[3]

Furthermore, the local authority used the 'resources' argument. It told me that under its care plan it would put considerable resources into a placement with the father, but that if I made a residence order in favour of the grandmother, even if I combined it with a supervision order, the same level of resources would not be made available.[4]

My second example was in fact the sequel to *Oxfordshire County Council v M*[5] a case in which there were siblings already in care under an order from the family proceedings court, and not therefore related in forensic terms to the child the subject of the application before me. However, what had happened to them was of critical relevance to the child with whom I was concerned and had to be investigated. During the course of that investigation, it transpired that the care plan for the children with whom I was not formally concerned had been changed subsequent to the making of the care orders relating to them – contrary to specific assurances given to the justices – and a course of action embarked upon by the local authority which both the consultant psychiatrist advising the authority and I thought quite contrary to their interests. Apart from expressing my concern to the Director of Social Services of the local authority in question, there was nothing I could do.

---

1 [1994] 2 FLR 423 at 427.

2 See the example given by Bracewell J at note 1 on p 6, *supra*.

3 One of several further ironies of this particular case was that placement of the child with the (social) father under a care order did not give him parental responsibility, whereas a residence order to the grandmother would have given it to her. By way of an aside I repeat my view that it is most unfortunate that the Children Act does not permit a third party to obtain parental responsibility for a child except through the medium of a residence order. The father in the case I am describing, and the grandmother in *Re W (A Minor) (Adoption: Mother under Disability)* [1995] Fam 120, who took all the decisions about her mentally disabled daughter's baby were both deserving of parental responsibility, and it is a defect in the Act that it is not broad enough to enable the court to confer parental responsibility where the court thinks the interests of the child require it.

4 An extension of the 'resources' argument in a more acute form is to be found in *Re C (Family Assistance Order)* [1996] 1 FLR 425, in which Johnson J was told by a local authority that it did not have the resources to implement a family assistance order made by the court under section 16 of the Act. The judge decided that there was nothing he could do that would be appropriate or sensible, except to admit failure. This is plainly highly unsatisfactory. See also the decision of the House of Lords in *In re C (A Minor) (Interim Care Order: Residential Assessment)* [1996] 3 WLR 1098, discussed in a different context in the text to note 1 on p 9.

5 [1994] Fam 151, CA.

Changing the care plan post care order

This latter case illustrates a further area of concern in which, in practical terms, both the parents of a child and the court are powerless. There is in the Act nothing to stop a local authority changing its care plan radically, sometimes within days of the care order being made.

I have now had several cases in which this has happened. In one, a resource thought to be available turned out not to be. This was not the local authority's fault, but as a result the child was not placed in a therapeutic unit and was left in an unsatisfactory short-term placement which, by drift, became long term.

In another case, a dramatic alteration in the child's placement was achieved by the local authority obtaining an order for the recovery of the child from the person with whom he had been placed under the care order and who refused to give him up. It subsequently transpired that the recovery order had been applied for on factual premises which were demonstrably wrong. The application for the recovery order was also contrary to the social workers' stated views as to the child's progress in the placement from which he was abruptly removed. But the circuit judge who heard the application under section 50 of the Children Act 1989[1] took the view, rightly, that he had no discretion to refuse to make the recovery order. The child was in care, the local authority had the right to exercise parental responsibility. Parliament in these circumstances has deprived the court of the discretion to investigate the local authority's decision to require the child to be moved.

In a third case the facts were that two children had been made the subject of a care order by the President in 1991 with a view to being placed for adoption. Not only did the local authority fail to place them for adoption: it transpired that in their first foster placement they were sexually abused and in their second subsequent foster placement (inappropriately chosen by the local authority) they were physically assaulted – assaults of sufficient severity to result in a prosecution of the foster mother.[2]

What remedy was open to the mother, who had remained in regular contact with the children? Only (1) to apply to revoke the care orders, and (2) to apply for contact. The latter was not in dispute: the former was a hopeless application, which I was constrained to dismiss. I was thus obliged by the Act simply and without more awaiting response to leave both children in the care of a local authority which had been responsible for greater abuse to the children than that which precipitated their admission to care.

In particular, I had no power to regulate what the local authority henceforth did with the children, or where or how they were placed. My only course was to send a copy of my judgment to the Director of Social Services for the authority concerned. Given that I was charged in the application to revoke the

---

1 Section 50 empowers the court to make orders, inter alia, enabling a local authority (which has parental responsibility for a child under a care order) to remove the child from anybody who has unlawfully (that is without the local authority's agreement) taken the child or is keeping him or her away from the placement selected by the local authority. It is clearly a necessary power for the court to have.

2 As the guardian ad litem put in her report:

> 'Having been given leave to place the children for adoption by the President of the Family Division in December 1991, [the local authority] for one reason or another had still failed to find any suitable adoptive parents by January 1993 when the present application for substitution of supervision orders for care orders was made to this court. Instead [the local authority] had placed the children with temporary foster carers who had been approved by a voluntary agency and by [the social services department of an adjoining authority], and who proved to be more abusive to these two children than [the mother] had ever been when she was regularly under the influence of alcohol. In addition, [the local authority] were unable to assess that the children were being abused until the abuse became quite blatant and could no longer be hidden, because the foster carer and her family went to some quite considerable lengths to prevent the children talking about the kind of care they were receiving.'

care order with making orders which were in the paramount interests of the welfare of the children, I regarded this as highly unsatisfactory.[1]

In the circumstances I have been describing, a parent's opportunity to challenge the local authority is limited in the extreme. Furthermore, such cases, to my mind, all demonstrate aptly the proposition that the court's wish to do what it perceives to be in the interests of the child is fettered by the restrictions on its powers imposed by the Act.[2]

The use of interim orders

The court's powers under interim orders, and in particular, the power to direct a residential assessment under section 38(6) have recently been helpfully clarified by the House of Lords in *In re C (A Minor) (Interim Care Order: Residential Assessment)*.[3] That was, however, a case in which interim orders were being used for the purposes for which they were primarily conceived, namely to assemble evidence for a final hearing. In the context of this paper, interim orders have been used for a different purpose.

There are cases in which interim care orders can properly be used at the end of what is planned to be a final hearing if, at that point, the judge is not satisfied that all the facts are as clearly known to the court as can be hoped. Two good examples of this approach are *C v Solihull Metropolitan Borough Council* and *Hounslow London Borough Council v A*.[4] In the former, a child who had been injured had been returned home by justices without a proper assessment of parental capacity to care for him. In the latter, justices made a care order when an application by a father for a residence order was outstanding and an assessment by the local authority of his capacity to care for the child was in progress but had not been completed. In both cases, it was clearly premature to make a final order, whether for care or residence.

Another good example of the proper use of interim orders is *Buckinghamshire County Council v M*.[5] In this case, the question for the judge was what should happen to the child. Was he to be adopted – the local authority's case – or was an attempt to be made at reuniting him with his mother – her case, supported by a distinguished child psychiatrist? The judge decided the latter was the right course. The plan which he wished to put into effect was that there should be a phased and structured scheme for rehabilitation of the child to his mother over the course of three months with a review at the end of that period.

Once it is appreciated (1) that the decision made by the judge (a) was not only a decision which he was fully entitled to make but (b) was one which Parliament had entrusted to him alone; and (2) that what the judge was doing was *not* making a final order but proposing a course of action which was to be

---

1 *Re MD and TD (Minors) (No 2)* (1994) 24 Fam Law 489 at 450.

'I also cannot but reflect that this case throws into sharp relief the only major defect in the operation and effect of the Children Act 1989 of which I have experience, and that is the loss of the power of the High Court to monitor the progress of children whom it has placed in care. The major virtue of section 7(2) of the Family Law Reform Act 1969 was that it prevented drift. A judge making an order such as that made by the President in the instant case and concerned to ensure that drift did not occur had the power to direct that the case be restored to his list after a given interval for progress to be reported to him and further directions to the local authority to be given. Such deadlines, in my experience, greatly concentrated the minds of the parties and local authorities and were a real safeguard against drift. I venture to think that had this not been a 'deemed care order' under the transitional provisions of the Children Act the drift which has in fact occurred in this would not have happened.

Neither the President nor anybody associated with the hearing in December 1991 knew, of course, that the children either had been or were to be the victims of sexual abuse in the household of [their first foster parent]. But once again, had the President's order been made under section 7(2) of the 1969 Act the fact of the abuse when it emerged in February 1992 would have been reported to the court, and in my judgment it is highly likely that the court would then have taken a decision to keep the case strictly under review. Had that occurred it is likely either that the abuse which the children suffered in the household of [their second foster parent] either would not have occurred or, at the very least, the anxieties about the placement with their second foster parents would have come to the attention of the court and thus been investigated fully at a much earlier stage. In my judgment the armoury of child protection has lost a powerful weapon with the abolition of the powers of the High Court in wardship to monitor and in some cases direct the actions of local authorities.'

2 There is, of course, the local authority's internal complaints procedure, and complaints may be made to the Local Government Ombudsman. Whilst in my limited experience local authorities operate such procedures conscientiously, neither form of redress addresses the particular issue, which is the need and capacity to impose an alteration to the care plan or a means of monitoring its implementation.

3 [1996] 3 WLR 1098.

4 This is the test adopted by Ward J in *C v Solihull Metropolitan Borough Council* [1993] 1 FLR 290 and by Booth J in *Hounslow London Borough Council v A* [1993] 1 FLR 702.

5 [1994] 2 FLR 702, CA.

reviewed at the end of three months, the case becomes readily understandable and fits into the pattern of *Solihull* and *Hounslow*.

In *Buckinghamshire*, the Court of Appeal held that the judge's actual decision about what should happen to the child was unimpeachable: he was plainly acting within his powers. His error was to think that he could put his decision about the child into effect by making 'no order'. As the Court of Appeal pointed out, this would have brought the proceedings to an end. There would then have been no jurisdiction to conduct the review by the court which was an essential part of the plan and which was a prerequisite to a final decision. Equally, as the decision of the Court of Appeal in *Re T (A Minor) (Care Order: Conditions)*[1] makes clear, the judge could not impose a condition on a full care order that the local authority put in place a programme of rehabilitation. The court under a full care order cannot make a local authority do something it is plainly opposed to doing; thus to make a full care order in such circumstances would have been an abdication of judicial responsibility and plainly wrong.

Since a full care order in *Buckinghamshire* would have been wrong and would plainly have frustrated the judge's purpose, the obviously appropriate course was to make an interim care order with a review at the end of three months. Then, if the rehabilitation was successful, the judge would probably make a residence order in favour of the mother: if it failed, he would in all probability make a care order and permit the local authority to implement its care plan by taking steps to place the child for adoption.

Thus if *Buckinghamshire* is perceived as the court using interim care orders as a means of completing an assessment of a particular course of action with a view to a final decision being made at the end of a short and finite period, the case is entirely consistent with *Solihull* and *Hounslow* and, for that matter, with my own decision in *Re J*.

I am quite satisfied that where on the hearing of an application for a care order there remains an issue to be decided between the parties which is properly within the judicial competence, it is an abnegation of judicial responsibility to delegate that decision to the local authority under a care order. At the same time, I respectfully agree with the Court of Appeal in *Re L*[2] that the power to make further interim orders should not be used artificially or as a means of exercising supervisory jurisdiction over matters which Parliament has entrusted to the local authority.

Discussion

I wish to make it clear that I am sure the cases I have been describing are a minority, although the underlying facts of each are in no sense unusual. I shall welcome input from the judges at the conference to see if their experience matches mine.

I should also make it clear that I do not believe that the courts should be given a general power to supervise the activities of local authorities. Such a power is undesirable in principle and would be unworkable in practice.

I do, however, think that some change in the law is necessary so that the progress of children in care can be monitored in cases where the judge perceives such a process to be necessary, or where the care plan goes wrong at an early stage. In either case the objective is for the court to be satisfied that the care plan upon which the child was placed in care is being properly implemented.

At a recent discussion amongst the designated judges at the annual President's conference, there was a general feeling that reform was required. I look forward to discussion at the conference as to how these objective can be achieved.[3]

---

1 [1994] 2 FLR 423.

2 [1996] 1 FLR 116 at 126.

3 The conference produced a number of valuable suggestions in the working groups into which the delegates were divided between plenary sessions. The results are printed at pp 94–96. The group of which I was a member (Group B) included a consultant psychiatrist, a director of social services, a guardian ad litem, a social worker and a senior retired official from the Department of Health. Our views are set out at p 94. We worked on the premise that primary legislation was unlikely in the immediately foreseeable future. Our proposals were, therefore, designed both to improve social work practice and, by means of collating the information from care cases over a two-year period, to ascertain the true extent of the problem. The identification of a named officer within the local authority to oversee the implementation of the care plan would, we thought, avoid drift. It was a matter of considerable satisfaction to me that such a group was, in a relatively short time, able to hammer out agreed proposals.

Absent primary legislation, one proposition which appeals to me is for the judge in an appropriate case (which I would anticipate would be the exception rather than the rule) to be given the power to extend the appointment of the child's guardian ad litem for a period of (say) 12 months with liberty to the guardian ad litem to restore the matter to the court if the care plan was not being implemented appropriately.

My experience of guardians is that they are the child's protection against bad social work practice, and could be relied upon to monitor those cases which had caused judicial anxiety. The question, of course, remains: what does the judge do if such a case comes back? In my view the judge in such circumstances would have to be given the power to require the local authority either to put forward a fresh care plan or to direct the local authority where to place the child.

In the meantime, however, judges and magistrates must all continue to work within the statutory framework. What, in practice, should we be doing? The answers, I think, are:

(a) strict scrutiny of local authority care plans;
(b) proactive examination in court of the areas of concern if they are not adequately investigated by the profession;
(c) invitations to local authorities to reconsider and reflect upon aspects of the care plan which the evidence shows to be inappropriate; and
(d) ultimately, a refusal to make a care order where the care plan is perceived by the court to be contrary to the interests of the child.

I recently put to a member of the Court of Appeal the dilemma: what do you do when a care order is inevitable because the parents are either abusive or hopeless and you feel that the local authority's plan for the child is a potential disaster but the local authority simply refuses to change it? The answer was: 'Go down fighting'. By this I think was meant – make the care order, give your judgement in open court, spell out your reasons for disagreeing with the care plan, and send a copy to the director of social services.

I agree that in the current state of the law this, in the unattractive modern phrase, is 'the bottom line'. But if this is the state of the law, it is profoundly unsatisfactory, particularly in a jurisdiction which is multi-disciplinary and in which the court wishes to engage, and indeed is dependent upon, the co-operation of those other disciplines.

I am happy to say, that although I have come near it, I have not, as yet, found myself in the position which I put to the member of the Court of Appeal. I hope I never do. I maintain my belief in the co-operative exercise between court, local authority and other agencies all seeking the best solution for the child. Unfortunately, it seems to me that the Act, as I have now already said at least twice, often hinders the process rather than enhances it, and specifically makes it sometimes impossible for judges to perform their statutory duty to make orders which they perceive to be in the best interests of the child.

APPENDIX 1

Re J (Minors) (Care: Care Plan)

(1) The power of the High Court to monitor care orders made in wardship or matrimonial proceedings, together with the power to give directions and require the case to return for further consideration and review by the court, has been specifically excluded by the Children Act 1989. As Butler-Sloss LJ put it in *Re B (Minors) (Care: Contact: Local Authority's Plans)* [1993] 1 FLR 543 at p 548:

> 'The earlier provisions have all been repealed. Section 100 excludes the wardship jurisdiction and the inherent jurisdiction of the High Court in respect of children to be placed in care or who are in care. Consequently, once a care order has been made, the court can no longer monitor the administrative arrangements for the child and has no say in those arrangements unless there is an application before the court.'

(2) Once a care order has been made, not only does the court no longer have any power to monitor the administrative arrangements for the child; there is no power to direct that the guardian ad litem continue his involvement in the case. Thus the guardian's involvement also ends when a care order is made: see *Kent County Council v C* [1993] Fam 57, [1993] 1 FLR 308.

(3) Before mading a care order under s 31 of the 1989 Act, the court must go through a two-stage process. The court must first be satisfied that the threshold criteria under s 3 have been met. Secondly, the court must be satisfied under s 1(5) of the Act that the making of a care order is better for the child than making no order. This involves considering the matters set out in s 1(2) and specifically, the 'check-list' set out in s 1(3) of the Act: see s 1(4). When considering the second stage of the process the court takes the child's welfare as its paramount consideration: see s 1 of the Act generally.

(4) The combination of the factors set out under (1) and (2) above requires the court carefully to scrutinise the care plan prepared by the local authority and to satisfy itself that the care plan is in the child's interests. Thus, if the court is not satisfied the care plan is in the best interests of the child, the court may refuse to make a care order.

(5) It follows that the care plan prepared by the local authority is an extremely important document. In *Manchester City Council v F, Note* [1993] 1 FLR 419, Eastham J stated that the care plan delivered by the local authority should accord, so far as is reasonably possible, with *The Children Act 1989 Guidance and Regulations* vol 3, chap 2, para 2.62 (*Family Placements*), prepared by the Department of Health and published by HMSO.

(6) The report of *Manchester City Council v F, Note* does not reproduce para 2.62 of vol 3 of the *Guidance and Regulations*. In the hope, therefore, that the criteia therein referred to will become better known in the profession, I propose to read the matters listed in para 2.62 in their entirety into this judgment. Whilst it is recognised in that paragraph that there is no prescribed format for the child care plan, the plan should be recorded in writing and contain the child's and his family's social history and the following key elements – and they are then listed:

> 'The child's identified needs (including needs arising from race, culture, religion or language, special education or health needs.)'

Next:

'– how those needs might be met;
– aim of plan and time-scale; the proposed placement (type and details);
– other services to be provided to child and/or family either by the local authority or other agencies;
– arrangements for contact and reunification;
– support in placement;
– likely duration of placement in the accommodation;
– contingency plan, if placement breaks down;
– arrangements for ending the placement (if made under voluntary arrangements);
– who is to be responsible for implementing the plan (specific tasks of overall plan);
– specific detail of the parents' role in day-to-day arrangements;
– the extent to which the wishes and views of the child, his parents and anyone else with sufficient interest in the child (including representatives of other agencies) have been obtained and acted upon and the reasons supporting this or explanations of why wishes/views have not been discounted;
– arrangements for input by parents, the child and others into the ongoing decision-making process;
– arrangements for making the responsible authority of disagreements or making representations;
– arrangements for health care (including consent to examination and treatment);
– arrangements for education; and dates of reviews.'

(7) Eastham J in *Manchester City Council v F, Note* (above) did not feel inclined to say that every care plan should contain evidence as to the feasibility of the long-term proposals made by the local authority. He was specifically dealing with a case in which the local authority was planning to place the child in question for adoption and was

thus concerned that evidence of long-term proposals would breach the duty of confidentiality. I will return to this point in a moment.

(8) In *C v Solihull Metropolitan Borough Council* [1993] 1 FLR 290, the test formulated by Ward J for the making of final care orders was that the court should make a final decision, finally disposing of the case only when all the facts were as clearly known to the court as could be hoped. At p 302B he said this:

> 'We have heard much, as we have prepared for the implementation of the Children Act 1989, about partnership. One of those partnerships is the very important one between the court and the local authority, where the part played by the court is to consider all the facts that are presented to it by the local authority and to make a decision finally disposing of the case when all of those facts are as clearly known to the court as could be hoped. That stage has not been reached in this case. The court does not know what the result of the assessment will be. For the court now to make a care order passes the responsibility of ultimate decision to the local authority in such a way as would perhaps unfairly preclude the parents and grandparents inviting the court to look at the result of the assessment before a final decision as to the placement of the child is made. The parents should not be left to apply for the discharge of a care order upon the only difficult ground available, namely that of making a residence order, for that might present the parents with an impossibly difficult task or certainly one which would be unfairly biased against them. It is for the local authority to put all material facts before the court, in this case the result of the assessment, before inviting the court to pass to them the huge responsibility of the management of a full care order. The court should be slow to abdicate its responsibility until all the facts are known. Therefore, a care order at this stage is quite inappropriate because it passes the control of the future of this child out of the hands of the court into the hands of the local authority and I am not prepared to do that. I hope that remarks of that kind will not cause affront to the local authority, whose role in these cases is crucial and upon whose support and help the court depends.
>
> There is, however, a third course open and that is to invoke the wide powers of the court to keep control of the case, to make interim arrangements and not to come to a final decision until it is right to do so. Those who practised in the High Court enjoyed the wide discretion the High Court had in exercising its wardship jurisdiction. That jurisdiction has gone as a remedy available to the local authority but the range of powers that the High Court had has not gone altogether. They are in very large measure preserved in the Act and are now available to all courts: county courts and magistrates' courts. The virtues of the flexibility of the wardship jurisdiction must now be recognised by the lower courts and insofar as the same flexibility can be achieved under the Children Act, the options available must be used to their full advantage. That is the message which this judgment seeks to deliver to the justices on this circuit and elsewhere.'

(9) In *Hounslow London Borough Council v A* [1993] 1 FLR 702, Booth J adopted the test laid down by Ward J in *C v Solihull MBC* when allowing an appeal from justices who had made a full care order at a time when an application for a residence order in the father's favour was outstanding and when an assessment by the local authority of his capacity to care for the child was in progress but had not been completed. In these circumstances Booth J adjourned the proceedings, made an interim care order and directed a further hearing once the local authority's assessment of the father had been completed. Booth J accepted that this course would involve delay but echoed the words of Ward J in *C v Solihull MBC* that although delay was ordinarily inimical to the welfare of the child, planned and purposeful delay might well be beneficial.

(10) In *C v Solihull MBC*, Ward J also dealt with the administrative means of dealing with the fact that interim care orders for care or supervision could last only 28 days. He cited r 28 of the Family Proceedings Courts (Children Act 1989) Rules 1991 (SI 1991/1395) which provide for continuations of interim orders by consent and without the attendance of the parties.

APPENDIX 2

Care Plans

1 Understanding and analysis of 'care plans' should include consideration of the Children Act 1989 and Regulations together with the *Children Act 1989 Guidance and Regulations* issued by HMSO and, in particular, Vol 3 'Family Placement' and Vol 4 'Residential Placement'.

The specific Regulations include:

Arrangements for Placement of Children (General) Regulations 1991;
The Foster Placement (Children) Regulations 1991;
The Placement of Children with Parents etc Regulations 1991;
Contact with Children Regulations 1991;
Review of Children's Cases Regulations 1991.

2 Neither the Statute nor the Regulations use the terminology 'care plan'. The statutory duty which is imposed upon local authorities is to 'so far as is reasonably practicable, make immediate and long term arrangements for that placement, and for promoting the welfare of the child who is to be placed' before the child is placed (Regulation 3(1), Arrangements for Placement of Children (General) Regulations 1991). There is an obligation to record those arrangements in writing (Regulations 3(5), ibid) and to maintain written case records which include a copy of the arrangements (Regulation 8(1), ibid). In relation to what matters are required to be recorded in those written arrangements, those are set out in Schedules 1, 2 and 3 to the Arrangements for Placement of Children (General) Regulations 1991.

3 The above duties imposed by the Regulations are statutory to the extent that they derive from a statutory instrument and, in consequence, the document produced as a result of the requirement to record the arrangements in writing must be regarded as a statutory document. It is on this basis that I disagree with the assertion made by Lady Justice Butler-Sloss in *Re L (Sexual Abuse: Standard of Proof)* [1996] 1 FLR 116 at 126 that the 'care plan' is not a statutory document.

4 It is my contention that confusion has arisen for courts and practitioners in relation to 'care plans' becuase there is no prescribed format for a 'care plan' and neither the Children Act nor the Regulations use the term. 'Care plan' is the shorthand term which has been adopted for convenience and ease of understanding by courts and practitioners alike to describe what has been assumed to be a 'forensic tool' rather than the 'social work tool' which the plan for the child is intended to be. I suspect that this has happened because practitioners have failed to undertake an analysis of the entire statutory framework when they have prepared arguments on issues relating to local authority planning. I assume this to be the explanation for no reference to citation of the relevant Regulations and Guidance being made in the cases which have been reported dealing with care plans which are:

Note: Manchester City Council v F [1993] 1 FLR 419;
Re J (Minors) (Care: Care Plan) [1994] 1 FLR 253;
Re S (A Minor) (Care: Contact Order) [1994] 2 FLR 222;
Re T (A Minor) (Care Order: Conditions) [1994] 2 FLR 423;
Re S and D (Children: Powers of Court) [1995] 2 FLR 456;
Re L (Sexual Abuse: Standard of Proof) [1996] 1 FLR 116.

5 The HMSO *Guidance*, Vol 3 'Family Placement', Ch 2, p 3, makes it clear that the expression 'arrangements' is intended to refer to 'plan'. It specifically refers in the HMSO *Guidance* to the social work term 'plan' being used when talking about 'arrangements'. Furthermore, in the introduction to Ch 2 of Vol 3, it is made clear that the 'regulations and guidance together with the regulations and guidance relating to specific types of placement provides a statutory framework within which responsible authorities should work with children and families and act as good parents'.

6 One of the problems for practitioners and others in looking at the different sets of regulations, is that the draftsmen have used the term 'arrangements' interchangeably so that in some contexts 'arrangements' refers to 'the plan' whilst elsewhere it clearly refers to 'practical arrangements' being made eg for the implementation of contact or implementation of medical examinations. The position is compounded because in the Placement of Children with Parents etc Regulations 1991, Schedule 2, a further element of inconsistency in terminology appears because reference is made to 'the Authority's plans'.

7 However, the confusion in terminology should not allow confusion to pervade understanding of the statutory obligations imposed upon local authorities to prepare 'care plans' from 'the earliest possible time after recognition of need or referral where the provision of accommodation (whether voluntary or compulsory) is likely to be necessary' (Vol 3 ibid, Ch 2, p 3). This provides the justification, in appropriate cases, for seeking a direction for the filing of the 'care plan' very early in the proceedings which then ensures that the court can quite properly indicate at an early stage whether the local authority's plan is likely to meet with approval.

8 My contention is that the 'care plan' should be seen and understood to be a 'social work tool' which is a dynamic document which should grow, be reviewed, revised and amended according to changes in the child's circumstances or those of his parents or other information obtained such as the outcome of assessments etc. The 'care plan' should form

part of the child's social services file. It is a document which should be added to or amended every time a review is held in accordance with the Regulations. The 'care plan' which is required to be filed with the court immediately prior to disposal of the proceedings is at best a 'snapshot' according to the circumstances of the child and parents which exist at that time. As such it should contain informed an authoritative statements of intent as to how the child's identified needs will be met for the foreseeable future.

Iain M Hamilton
19 November 1997

FIRST SESSION: DISCUSSION IN RESPONSE TO MR JUSTICE WALL'S PAPER

There was some concern expressed as to what form any involvement of the court post-care order would take. The suggestion that the court might get involved in cases which 'went wrong' begged the question of what that actually meant. What would a review of a particular case after the making of a care order achieve in practice? Are the problems encountered in the implementation of care plans amenable to judicial intervention or is one simply substituting one judgment on very difficult and complex situations for another which may not necessarily be any better? It was also suggested that there would be considerable difficulty in deciding what would be the criteria to be satisfied before bringing a case back to court after the making of the care order.

There was broad consensus amongst the judiciary that the difficult cases were those in which all the appropriate information/evidence necessary for the making of a care order had been obtained but the judge was adamantly opposed to the care plan put forward by the local authority. In such circumstances, at present the judge has no choice but to make the care order despite concerns about the proposed plan. It was suggested that it was at this crucial stage in proceedings that the judge lost his or her ability to make the decisions about a child's welfare.

There was general agreement that all involved in this area of work would appreciate knowing more of the outcomes for the children made the subject of care orders. It was suggested that one could look for research purposes at those cases in which a judge had had to make findings and decide contested care cases and follow what happened to those children after the making of an order. However, it was noted that it was potentially difficult to assess what correlation there was between the making of the care order and the outcome for the particular child. Clearly, other factors could and frequently would intervene, making it difficult to assess the link between outcomes and the original decision made.

SECOND SESSION

MEDICAL INPUT TO CARE PLANNING: THE CONTRIBUTION OF CHILD AND ADOLESCENT MENTAL HEALTH SERVICES (CAMHS) TO THE CARE PLANNING PROCESS

Dr Claire Sturge

SUMMARY OF PAPER

Specificity of Care Plans

Dr Sturge introduced her paper by emphasising the need for greater inter-agency partnership, suggesting it would be of assistance if greater use were made of CAMHS knowledge at the planning stage. She felt that it was important to see the Care Plan as an overview of a child at a particular point in time and that such plans should be highly specific to that child's needs and carefully reasoned as to how such needs might be met within it. Such specific plans would have the advantage of providing continuity for the child in situations where, for example, there was a change of social worker. These plans should include measurable objectives to ensure that one was able to assess precisely whether these are achieved and on which one can base management decisions, for example, to abandon a rehabilitation plan. Time-scales in the plan should be such that any drift is immediately identifiable.

Accountability

Dr Sturge considered that there was a real problem with Care Plans in that it was questionable what purpose they served if no one was accountable for them. She expressed the view that their importance was often undervalued by judiciary and social workers alike; judges were concerned with their 'lack of control'; social workers often saw them as 'a necessary chore'. She expressed a belief that the amount of thought put into its preparation and the clarity of the Care Plan is often the child's best safeguard for the future. There was something very wrong in a system in which no one is accountable for such plans. She felt that it was important to know what review mechanisms, both internal and external, were available and what circumstances would trigger an external 'audit' of a Care Plan. She also emphasised the need to avoid delay, reduce the number of moves of children in care and ensure the involvement of the child, its parents and siblings in the Care Plan.

Introduction

While not directly the remit of CAMHS, like others involved in promoting children's welfare, we have some general concerns in relation to Care Planning.

These are:

- The need for greater inter-disciplinary partnership at all stages of the Care Planning process.
- The concerns throughout our professions about the follow-through of Care Plans ie the lack of judicial or other outside review of the implementation of Care Plans or of major changes in Care Plans.
- The advantages of 'threshold hearings' when the main work in drawing up a Care Plan with the family can be done only after a finding has been made. However, careful timetabling is necessary not to make a nonsense of the two stages.

  The Scottish Children's Panels, as a disposal process, has certain advantages, and how best to manage very difficult situations needs to remain an open issue, drawing on othe systems where appropriate.

- Enormous concerns that the frequent and sometimes unnecessary moves of children in the care system do irreparable damage to children's mental health and emotional development. We are, therefore, greatly interested in any ideas that address ways of reducing uncertainty and moves for children, eg concurrent placements.
- The impact of delay, uncertainty and drift on children in the court system. Delays are as great as ever and the time-keeping aspect of the guardian ad litem's role has failed.
- The general standard of Care Plans (see below).
- After considering the physical safety of children, consideration of how to promote their mental welfare is of utmost importance. The body of this paper deals with how child and adolescent mental health specialists can contribute to promoting mental health in the Care Planning process.

SPECIFIC ROLES FOR CHILD AND ADOLESCENT MENTAL HEALTH SERVICE PROFESSIONALS

This will be considered in three sections:

(1) The stage leading up to the formulation of a Care Plan.
(2) The formulation of the Care Plan.
(3) The implementation of the Care Plan.

1 LEADING UP TO THE FORMULATION OF A CARE PLAN

Knowledge and expertise which can contribute to the Care Planning process

Assessment in relation to Care Planning

Areas that should be covered in an expert's report and which can inform the drawing up of the Care Plan:

- *Issues intrinsic to the child.* Individual assessment leading to psychiatric/psychological formulation including developmental, emotional, social, behavioural, cognitive and educational functioning.

  Note: Child mental health experts can help distinguish between causes intrinsic to the child and environmental causes of which parenting is the most relevant. The outcome for the child is the result of the interaction between the intrinsic and environmental.

  Some parents might be 'good enough' to parent children with no major developmental problems but cannot meet the special needs of a child with them.

  Children also bring their own temperamental characteristics into the situation and some children are born with more difficult temperaments, putting strain on any parent (Thomas and Chess). Temperamental differences, together with early experiences, will affect their resilience in the face of adversity (Fonagy).

  The needs of children with specific disorders are best met by particular types of management and care.

- *Children on the autistic continuum.* There is a body of research now on how such children are best managed.

- *Children with learning difficulties/developmental problems.* There is no fundamental difference in planning for these children and difficulties in planning arise mainly from associated behaviour problems, eg challenging behaviours. Severely retarded children present more particular demands in terms of caring.

  The vulnerability of such children to abuse – physical and sexual – within the care framework needs to be borne in mind in planning.

  Careful assessment during the Court and Care Planning process often greatly assists these children in identifying in a detailed way their specific needs and ensuring these are met, eg within the educational system.

- *Children with attentional problems and conduct disorders – 'disruptive children'.* These children require particular care – the importance of warm regard with a low level of criticism, of consistent, calm discipline and routines, of close supervision is now well-established. Foster carers/prospective adopters vary greatly in their skills in these areas. It needs to be remembered that such problems in conduct-disordered children is largely attributable to the children's past care, ie deficient parenting. In children with attentional problems, the quality of parenting contributes to the degree of dysfunction the child exhibits.
- *Traumatised children.* There is increasing knowledge of how best to help such children depending very much on the experiences of the individual child. The issues in relation to contact between a traumatised child who has been removed and his or her abuser is a complex one. Whether or not contact of some sort is likely to facilitate the child's recovery from the trauma and general development, particularly self-esteem and identity, need careful consideration.

Overall, the important contribution a CAMHS specialist has to make is in her/his knowledge of the relative importance of the placement and of treatment across different situations – for example, in some disorders, the type of placement is all-important with any forms of therapy having relatively little to offer. The CAMHS specialist can bring to bear his or her knowledge of the likely prognosis for the particular problem that the child presents, predict about the child's development and future needs, and what will and will not provide ameliorating circumstances.

Issues to do with relationship problems

Problems arising out of disturbed or disordered infant-carer or child-carer relationships brings another dimension in terms of children's needs.

Below is one way of conceptualising a gradation of such relationship problems (Anders 1989):

Relationship perturbation (the mildest form)

- Transient disruptions in environment including minor physical illnesses.
- Satisfactory family and social supports.
- Short duration (usually one month or less).

Relationship disturbance

- Pattern of inappropriate or insensitive regulation in interaction.
- Interaction patterns no rigidly fixed.
- Regulatory dysfunction confined to one domain of interaction.
- Moderate duration (usually one to three months).

Relationship disorder (the most severe form)

- Pattern(s) of inappropriate or insensitive regulation in interaction.
- Interaction patterns are fixed and not easily altered.
- Developmental milestones of one or both partners disrupted.
- Regulatory dysfunction is more likely to be pervasive across several interactional contexts and functional domains.
- Long duration (usually three months or more).

Such problems distort young children's development, affecting particularly their ability to:

- explore from a secure base;
- relate to and trust others;

- deal with stress or danger;
- regulate their behaviour.

The vast majority of cases coming to court fall in the severe end of these problems – the disorders.

These problems are also known as attachment problems or disorders.

Understanding of these relationship problems allows for a limited prediction about the quality of the child's future relationships and factors that will ameliorate the problems as well as information about the likely success (prognosis) of effecting sufficient change for the child to remain with or be returned to the natural carer.

For example, a recent study of adoption (D Howe) showed how a good 'early start' predicted a better outcome even with somewhat later adoptions.

There are specific situations where a very different type of Care Plan may be required (see next section). Problems intrinsic to the parent can have devastating effects on the child and the relationship between them.

Problems intrinsic to the carer or the carer's situation – adult risk factors

- Parental mental illness.
- Alcohol and substance misuse.
- Domestic violence.
- Parental criminality.

Dr Glaser's and Ms Prior's recent research on children registered for emotional abuse confirms the importance of the first three. The Review of Part 8 reviews by P Falcov, while underlining the risk factors associated with parental mental health, indicates the need for further more detailed research.

Child psychiatrists, with the combination of their training in adult psychiatry and their knowledge of relationship and attachments issues, are well placed, with their adult colleagues, to address children's needs where a parent is mentally disordered.

CAMHS professionals can contribute in relation to the other three on the basis of their experience, knowledge and assessment but do not have unique expertise in relation to these problems.

Care Plans in these situations raise particular issues because the following need to be taken into account:

Mental disorders

Mental illness

- The prognosis and likely course of the parent's illness.
- The ill parent's insight into and understanding of his/her illness is critical and, linked to this, his or her ability to seek help when ill.
- The particular needs of the child resulting from the parent's mental illness, eg distorted reality.
- Genetic loading in the child.
- Family support systems: presence of a 'well' parent or family member.

With a mentally ill parent, the issues to do with whether such a person can parent may be quite different from issues involved in contact with that person.

Other problems

Personality disorders

These can have just as major an impact on the child's well-being and development. The parent's own experience of attachment may be particularly important. Prognosis for change often depends on testing this out as much as theoretical information based on research.

Munchausen by proxy/factitious illness

In addition to the features of the syndrome itself which can present significant risk to the child, there is the risk to children of doctors being induced to do unnecessary investigations and treatment. With young children, the doctors are relatively powerless as the doctor relies on the history provided by the carer and cannot afford to ignore this and not to investigate and treat.

The causes of such behaviours in carers is various and it should not be seen as a unitary syndrome. Such causes include genuine anxiety about illness, delusions about illness, an over-dependence or hallowing of doctors, a hostility and wish to rubbish doctors, the need for a specific role and for medical attention in which the child is, in effect, disregarded and used as an accessory to the malingering end of the spectrum where the motivation is financial gain, eg disability allowance. This makes for very complex situations in which Care Plans need tailoring to the specific circumstances.

Substance misuse

- The chances of the parent succeeding in becoming substance-free (and difficulties in predicting this).
- The social context of the parent: potential for social life independent of the substance misuse; support systems.
- The child's difficulty in understanding the situation, experiencing for much of the time a fluctuating quality of care and not accepting the need for alternative care.

Domestic violence/criminality

- The central issue here is often one of predicting the victim-parent or non-criminal parent's ability to separate permanently from the aggressor.
- The child may have a good relationship with one or both parents, find the situation 'acceptable' and may not accept the need for change.

These issues affect:

- The assessment of the risk situation.
- The time-scale within the Care Plan for attempting to effect change.
- Managing the child's resistance to alternative care and family loyalty including contact problems.
- Contact.

Parents with learning difficulties are not included here because we do not see the assessment of their parenting as intrinsically different from those of parents without such disabilities. The parent's ability to meet the child's needs must be assessed: their intellectual limitations may or may not affect this. A possible exception is parents with specific problems in addition to learning difficulties, eg Asperger's Syndrome where assessment would particularly examine the parent's ability to empathise with the child and be sensitive to the child's having his or her own individual mind with thoughts and feelings.

Developmental factors/siblings

CAMH professionals can contribute to the thinking and planning in relation to age/developmental-level specific issues, eg timing of change in infancy, contact issues in infancy including sibling contact. They may have a contribution in terms of the suitability of different family contexts, eg single parent, presence of other children. For example, the presence of another same-age child in the family has been shown to be associated with a greater risk of breakdown (Howe, 1997).

Our disciplines have strong views on the advantages of sibling groups remaining together as enhancing some aspects of the children's development. CAMHS professionals may have advice, based on the needs and functioning of different siblings and on joint assessment of their interactions and relationships, about whether joint or separate placement is required. They can advise, when separate placement is indicated, how best to manage the separations. However, other professionals, eg family placement experts, often have extensive experience of such matters.

Physical and mental disorders in the child

The prognosis and emotional impact of such disorders, both on the child and the carers, should be considered by the 'expert'.

Issues in relation to handicap, chromosomal abnormalities, genetic factors, HIV infection, presence of psychiatric disorders, or presence or possibility of developing severe mental illness all come into this.

2 THE ACTUAL FORMULATION OF THE CARE PLAN

If a CAMH professional has acted in a specialist or expert capacity in the assessment process leading up to care proceedings, then that person should expect to be consulted about the actual Care Plan. A disagreement between the 'expert' and the local authority social workers over such a plan should result in a meeting designed to resolve or clarify differences in much the same way that disagreeing experts are expected to do. This, of course, means the Care Plan must be drawn up several weeks before the hearing and not tabled at the hearing.

Specific areas of input from a CAMH expert

Clarity of the plan

Is the plan laid out in a way that:

- identifies the child's needs in a particular area;
- indicates how the plan meets those needs;
- makes clear how, whether or not the plan is succeeding in meeting those needs, it is to be monitored;
- expresses a view about what types of placement are suitable and why, and how the issue of siblings will be managed.

In particular, the Care Plan must make clear what is a priority for the particular child in question as against the 'dogma' that is produced in relation to any child. We would go as far as to suggest a different typeface or italics to emphasise this. For example, an over-riding priority may be for the child to be placed with his or her sibling rather than that it be in a family of the identical ethnic background.

Often the plan is clear about the child's needs in relation to placement but not so clear and specific in other areas, eg:

(a) *Plans aiming at returning the child home.* The changes necessary for this to be effected need to be clear and measurable. The basis on which decisions will be made needs to be operationalised with clear targets which can be evaluated objectively. An example might be, in a plan involving the aim of a return home – 'if at the end of three months, Mrs X is unable to acknowledge the need', time-limited stages are needed and flow charts may help in clarifying what contingency plans will come in when and under what circumstances.

(b) *Contact.* The aim and purpose of contact is rarely delineated. There is often an assumption, supposedly based on the Children Act, that contact should always be afforded and plans are often defensive, ie make clear why contact is being restricted but not what it is meant to achieve.

In considering contact, direct contact should be classified according to whether or not another adult is to be present (for which the unsatisfactory term 'supervised' is used to cover many things) and, if so, for what purpose – to protect the child, to manage the contact, to assess the contact, or to do a piece of work with the carer and the child.

CAMH specialists can contribute to issues around the role of contact or different levels of an ongoing relationship with a natural relative in their emotional development.

(c) What specific forms of explanation and support the child will be offered through the period of implementation and change.

(d) The child's attitude to the Care Plan and how the child will be involved in informing the review of progress of the Care Plan.

There are issues around:

- Parents who have played highly negative roles eg in abuse or in killing the other parent. Contrary to popular belief, the more 'negatively' the parent is perceived, the more difficult that makes it for the child to integrate his life story and inheritance in a coherent way and it is often all the more important for such children to experience that the 'bad' parent contains some good.
- Unreliable parent or parents who undermine placement.
- Ill parents who may present bizarrely.
- Parents who present superficially very well and make the child question why they are away.
- Siblings and other relatives.

Therapy: professional network support systems

Therapy and treatment are used here synonymously and defined as any direct intervention using specific techniques that might influence the prognosis for mental health in later life.

This distinguishes it from management of the child's care which is indirect and day-to-day care of the child although this can involve elements of a specific therapeutic type.

Therapy, in the sense defined, can be carried out by anyone with skills in therapy – social workers, care workers, foster carers in addition to CAMHS staff. Indeed, social workers are usually best placed to offer several different types of intervention in the child's interests.

Care Plans need to contain details of future professional input across agencies.

Any CAMH expert should, in their report, comment on therapeutic needs and how these might be timed and arranged in order to inform the Care Plan.

When recommending treatment following an assessment, the specialist should:

(a) Indicate what the treatment needs are considered to be at the time of that person's assessment (these may change).
(b) Make clear the particular aims of treatment.
(c) Make clear the means of treatment and how the treatment process might achieve the aims.
(d) Consider the timing and time-scale.
(e) Consider the practicalities including availability of services.
(f) Offer an argument to indicate the pros and cons of different types of intervention or management that have been considered. Where appropriate, this should be on an evidence-base of the relevant literature. Clear advantages of certain types of intervention have now been shown – for example, in conduct disorders, in post-traumatic stress disorders, in eating disorders, obsessive-compulsive disorders etc. In such instances, it is not just opinion but evidence that should guide treatment recommendations.

Feasibility of Care Plans

The CAMH professional may be able to usefully comment on how feasible a Care Plan is. In particular, on the feasibility of any therapeutic plan within it – local resources and ability to implement any therapy. The CAMH professional can look into the qualifications, training support and supervision of those offering therapy in the independent sector, eg in specialised children's home. These are often unsatisfactory.

The overall context of support offered in the placement also needs scrutiny, particularly with a disturbed youngster. Even when therapy is not indicated or not at that time, access to consultation and support from a local child and adolescent mental health service is often needed but not always available.

3 IMPLEMENTATION OF THE CARE PLAN

The following are only occasionally considered and can, in some situations, be helpful:

(1) Using the expert in the proceedings as an 'outside' consultant within the Care Plan, eg a contingency of a placement breaks down, or a time target is not reached. Remuneration needs to be sorted out.
(2) Building in the local child and adolescent mental health services, eg for a role as in (1) above, and for inclusion in some or all of a Care Plan. This would be particularly pertinent with a child already known to them or where there is a significant psychiatric problem in the child.

General comment

Much might be learnt from individual education plans and statements: when of high calibre, specify short- and long-term targets, have in-built review procedures with notification if there needs to be a formal reassessment of the plan and clear indications of who is doing what in the different agencies.

The child as the centre of the assessment, court and care planning process

This is being directly addressed by Ms Kenrick but, for completeness, the following areas need to be considered:

- The effects of and meaning to the child of the assessment.
- The undermining effects of uncertainty.
- Delay and the impact of this on the child being able to progress developmentally, particularly in their emotional development and relationships.

Support for the child during the process. Consideration of therapeutic help during the period of uncertainty if this can clearly bridge across the next change for the child. Any support offered during a transitional process must offer support to the child over current uncertainties and realities and not be seen as a vehicle for dealing with or resolving issues and problems of the past.

Involvement of the child in formulating the Care Plan. This needs consideration with any child able to understand this at all and should be an integral part of the planning with older children. The more the child is involved in developing the plans for him or her, the greater the likelihood that he or she will understand these and feel some ownership of them and investment in them. Appendix 1 to this paper contains a list of issues that can be useful in how to weight children's views.

The process of involving them in the review of Care Plans could be greatly developed: if short- and medium-term targets were clear in such plans, older children could usefully be part of assessing whether targets have been reached.

Ensuring the child has the necessary information at the time decisions are made and later

Informing the child of court decisions. Specific techniques can be used in informing even quite young children. A document should be drawn up at the time of the court's decision (and in situations where there is no judgment because agreement is reached) of what decisions were made and why. Similarly, the Care Plan could be outlined or attached. This would become the property of the child. In this way, the child would have access at all times and, in the case of a very young child, when the information would have meaning to him or her, to absolutely central information about themselves, and the reasons for their situations.

If this became set practice, judges might want to consider dictating a short document of this sort. Potentially, this could be one of the most important contributions social workers or courts could make to a child's future mental health.

There are concerns that 'life story work' is not always planned in an informed way in the child's best interest. It can just become a repository of conflicting or irrelevant information (see Appendix 2 to this paper).

Judges and guardians ad litem have an important role in explaining decisions to older children, especially where: (1) these are unwelcome; or (2) where the child needs decisions to be emphasised or symbolised because of their importance or validation of the child's position.

Placement breakdown/frequent moves/change of social worker. While contingency plans are required in relation to the first of these three, little is ever said about how the child will be helped through any of these events. The very reason the child is in care, or the continuity of the Care Plan, may be lost through such changes.

Care Plans should contain some in-built mechanism for sounding alarm bells over multiple moves, eg a plan could contain a statement such as if there are more than two moves for this child in the next year, a crisis planning meeting will be convened involving an outside Consultant. Ideally, such a mechanism might allow for a return to court for a reassessment of the Care Plan.

General comment

Courts should be wary of accepting Care Plans when the expert(s) in the case has/have not been involved in their formulation or which are seen as flawed by the expert(s). An obvious way forward in those situations would be for there to be a meeting to look at the differences between the expert(s) and the local authority (in a similar way to how differences between experts are currently addressed).

Threshold hearings

CAMH specialists favour these in general where there is a dispute as to fact. This is because:

- Threshold hearings give time between the two parts for meaningful consideration by parents of the threshold decisions and time to adjust to these.
- Often the best form of Care Plan cannot be devised until the reactions of the parents to the decision are known.
- Threshold hearings offer, in certain circumstances, a more appropriate period for the CAMH specialist to assess the parents and the situation (or offer consultation about this) free of any perception by the parents of a partisan role in the threshold proceedings.
- All the factors will contribute to a more realistic and informed Care Plan with less speculation.

Concurrent placements

CAMHS staff are extremely interested in these ideas. With the moving around of children as the single most frequently abusive experience in care, any way of reducing or eliminating this would be an important addition to protecting their emotional welfare. The reservations that social services are bound to feel in terms of what this demands of carers who may at the same time be adopters and what impact this may have on recruitment, the care system should be one which puts the best interests of children first and clearly before those of carers or difficulties for the system.

FUTURE SUGGESTIONS

Research

This is being dealt with in a separate section of the conference. There is a dearth of information. Particular areas are:

- Implementation and outcome of Care Plans.
- Impact of different contact arrangements.
- Outcome of Care Plans aiming at the child's return home: what proportion succeed and in what circumstances?
- Concurrent placements.
- Adoption versus long-term fostering.
- Outcome where an additional 'disruption' of attachment is involved.
- In relation to the individual needs of the child, eg is adoption of greater importance for neglected children?

- What proportion of long-term foster placements offer life-long support.
- Attachment status and its predictive value in relation to children's progress in the care system.
- Which children do better in more institutional settings.
- Follow-up in relation to different ways of managing/placing sibling groups.

OUR DISCIPLINES

Possible ways forward

(1) Should 'good practice' guidelines be drawn up for child and adolescent mental health professionals, based along the lines of this paper and lessons learnt at the conference?
(2) There is a need for relevant literature lists in relation to Care Planning issues or means of facilitating literature searches in relation to these to be available for mental health professionals.
(3) Evidence-based reviews of current literature on outcomes in different types of placements needs to be undertaken.

REFERENCES

Anders, T F (1989) *Clinical syndromes, relationship disturbances and their assessment* in Sameroff and Emde (eds). Relationship disorders in early childhood (New York, Basic Books) pp 125–144.

Black, D, Wolkind, S and Harris-Hendricks, J (eds) (1989) *Child Psychiatry and the Law* (Gaskell: Royal College of Psychiatrists).

Bowlby, J (1988) *A secure base: Clinical applications of attachment theory* (London, Routledge).

Brazelton and Cramer (1990) *The earliest relationship* (New York: Addison Wesely).

Duniz, M et al (1996) 'Changes in psychopathology of parents of non-organic failure to thrive infants during treatment' *European Child and Adol Psych* 5: 93–100.

Eekalaar (1996) *Child Abuse and Neglect* No 20 p 1123.

Falcov, A (1996) *Fatal child abuse and parental psychiatric disorder. Working together. Part 8 Reports.* Department of Health ACPC Series No 1 (London: HMSO).

Fonagy, P, Steele, M, Steel, H, Higgitt, A and Target, M (1994) 'The theory and practice of resilience' *J Child Psychol Psychiat* Vol 35, No 2, pp 231–257.

Glaser, D and Lynch, M A (1997) *Emotional abuse: Suspicion, investigation and registration* (Department of Health: due to be published).

Harder, D W (1980) 'Child competence and psychiatric risk relationships of parent, diagnostic classification and parent psychopathology: severity to child functioning' *Journal of Nervous and Mental Diseases* No 186 pp 343–347.

Horner, T and Guyer, M (1993) 'Infant placement and custody' in *Handbook of Infant Mental Health* Zeenah C H (ed) (Guildford Press) pp 462–479.

Howe D (1997) 'Parent-reported problems in 211 adopted children: some risk and protective factors' *J Child Psychol Psychiat* Vol 38, No 4 pp 401–412.

Katz, L (1996) 'Permanency action through concurrent planning' *Adoption and Fostering* Vol 20, No 2 pp 8–13.

Katz, L and Robinson, C (1991) *Foster care drift: a risk assessment matrix* (Child Welfare League of America) pp 347–358.

Livingston, R, Lawson, L and Jones, J (1993) 'Predictors of self-reported psychopathology in children abused repeatedly by a parent' *J Am Acad Child Adolesc Psychiatry* Vol 32, No 5 pp 948–953.

Mitchell, G (1996) *Care and contact plans – a Guardian's view*, Selected seminar papers (1994/95) (Legal Group AGM Seminar). *Interference or rubber stamp? The function of the court in child care cases 1995* (BAAF: Skyline House, London) pp 39–46.

Oates, M (1997) 'Patients as parents: the risk to children' *B J of Psychiat* 170 (suppl 2) pp 22–27.

Quinton, D (1984) 'Parental psychiatric disorder: effects on children' *Psychological Medicine* 14 pp 853–880.

Smith, C (1996) *The Local Authority: Responsibility and accountability in child care planning* Selected seminar papers (1994/95) (Legal Group AGM Seminar). *Interference or rubber stamp? The function of the court in child care cases 1995* (London: BAAF: Skyline House) pp 48–55.

Stern, D (1995) *The motherhood constellation* (New York: Basic Books).

Thomas, A and Chess, S (1977) *Temperament and development* (New York: Brunel/Maze).

Justice Wall (1996) *Constructive criticism or over-zealous investigation? The court's role in relation to the Local Authority Care Plan* Selected seminar papers (1994/95) (Legal Group AGM Seminar). *Interference or rubber stamp? The function of the court in child care cases 1995* (London: BAAF: Skyline House) pp 31–38.

APPENDIX 1

Considering children's wishes and feelings

Eekelaar draws attention to the many practical difficulties such an approach encounters. There are difficulties due to:

- Distinguishing between wishes and deeper feelings.
- Statements influenced by a specific context.
- Separating out the incidental or transitory.
- Pressure from disputing adults.
- Risk of being burdened with guilt.
- Risk of receiving hostility from others.
- Decision affected by information quality and provider bias.
- Articulation affected by age and how they might think it will be received.
- Whether they have promised someone what or not to say.
- Whether they have support.
- Where and how they are asked.
- Where it is difficult to explain the alternatives to children.

APPENDIX 2

Life story books

Children will 'normally' have access to an information or memory bank that they can tap into for information at appropriate times in their developmental years. That information may be accessed in response to needs that arise for the child.

Where a child is dislocated from their birth parents who represent their heritage or early carers who are information banks for early years, a life story book is a valuable source of the information.

However, children who are insecure may inadvertently have pressed on them threatening information about the circumstances of their infancy and behaviour of adults. That represents for the child a forced 'anamnesis'. In the Care Plan, there should be a statement of the means by which the story book data would be available to the child, in a way that is responsive to the child's needs, when the suitable time arises.

CARE PLANNING: THE EXPERIENCE OF THE CHILD

Jenny Kenrick

SUMMARY OF PAPER

Ms Kenrick introduced her paper by explaining that she had used a single case for study in order to elucidate thoughts about the more general context in which her work as a child psychotherapist within a multidisciplinary team takes place.

She noted that in some fields of research there was a return to the individual case study as a valid and complementary alternative to the larger more 'scientific' studies. In her own psychanalytic field, from Freud on, the individual case study has elicited theory that could usefully be applied over a wider clinical field. She firmly believed that the experience of one child can help to clarify some of the important issues for many other children.

Ms Kenrick stressed that throughout what she had written was her interest in good practice issues. Also, she thought it was helpful if one could pull out factors which lead to successful outcomes. In her experience, social workers were often better at doing this than clinicians who, by definition, most often become involved with children and their caring networks when things start to go wrong.

Further, a great value of interdisciplinary conferences such as this was that they may help those involved to find ways to work across professional disciplines to more truly co-operative and collaborative work. She supported the suggestions of Dr Claire Sturge for the early involvement of mental health professionals in planning for children and in remaining involved in such a way as to provide continuity in keeping the child in mind. This can be very difficult through multiple changes of placement and possibly of social worker – who does manage to keep the child in mind?

Turning to the specific case history in her paper, Ms Kenrick said that Kerry's history did point to drift in the system.

(1) *Decisions about* contact *delayed the process. Contact had been picked up for discussion by other conference members in their papers. The Children Act 1989 seemed to have had a major influence by slowing down the decision-making process whilst contact issues were decided. Are these delays in the interest of the parent or child?*

(2) The late involvement of child and adolescent mental health professionals *(4–5 years) in spite of indications of difficulties in Kerry's behaviour.*

(3) The precariousness of her world. *The need that children like Kerry have for* extraordinary internal resources *to manage changes of placement and in the circumstances of their life; also to survive demands for attachment and disruption of attachment.*

(4) *The real* difficulty of therapeutic work with children in transition. *Such children bring enormous distress and anger to those who work with them, including sometimes enduring actual physical attack. It is in this area that Ms Kenrick was very aware of the real difficulty of the social work position, having to make decisions where no one really does know the answers at a time when there is a real lack or resources.*

Ms Kenrick went on to say that there was valuable support in this difficult area from research. She cited examples in her field of two areas of research in 'promoting thinking about thinking', and about the contribution that that capacity to think can make in the mental health of the individual.

(1) *Attachment theory research: Ms Kenrick cited in particular the work of Peter Fonagy, Miriam Steele and others, who have made links between parents' attachment patterns and those of their children. Amongst the many useful conclusions to emerge from this research was that one of the things that matters, even where early experiences have been adverse, was the adult's capacity to go on thinking about those experiences; not to act out or pass on the impact of such experiences to the next generation, but to have some capacity to 'metabolise them'. This research was also demonstrting that if one can intervene in a child's destructive scenario early enough, he may be able to take better advantage of new situations offered to him.*

(2) *Neurological research: Ms Kenrick referred to the work of Bruce Perry and others in the United States with traumatised children. Such work had shown the impact of trauma, particularly during the early stages of development, on the growth of the neural pathways of the brain and the defensive behaviour patterns that can develop in the interests of survival. It had also shown, however, that if things change early enough, such adverse patterns can be repaired by later good experience.*

Ms Kenrick ended by saying that these areas of research were encouraging in that they demonstrated that therapeutic interventions were important and could make an impact for the long-term well-being of the children treated. In particular, with reference to the central theme of the conference, that such interventions could affect placement outcomes – a real endorsement for the therapeutic endeavours of those involved in the field.

At the Tavistock Clinic we have an Adoption and Fostering workshop. This provides a multidisciplinary group of practitioners with a forum in which they can discuss their cases. Because these are the cases that are the most complex and most need discussion they are often those where things do not seem to be going well for the child or children concerned. We also listen to presentations of research in hand, and we discuss together themes that emerge. We share our experience and strive to develop our expertise.

For the purposes of this paper I wish to focus on the experience of the children that we refer to as children 'in transition'. These are children who are being 'looked after' by a local authority, for whom there will be a Care Plan, to which the clinician may or may not have contributed. These are children who have not yet been placed permanently in an adoptive home or in a long-term foster care placement which is expected to endure until the child leaves Care. Again and again we are dispirited by how long many children stay 'in transition' and by how many moves of placement some of them have had, too frequently into double figures and sometimes numbering between 15 and 20 moves before the child has reached secondary school age.

I am writing as a child psychotherapist, a clinician who works with children, engaging them in the struggle to explore and to understand their individual internal world, the 'inner representations' of self and others. From there the struggle is to comprehend how these may have influenced what each child has made of earlier experiences and is making of present experiences. For even when circumstances seem to be more favourable things may still not go well for these children – earlier patterns of expectation or of behaviour may persist, sometimes almost inexplicably for those who care for the child. At the same time, it is crucial that we pay full attention to the current external realities of a child's life because of the impact that these have on the child's internal world. There is a continuing and complex and dynamic interaction between internal and external. With children who may have been abused and whose parents may have been unable to look after them for reasons of physical or mental illness, for example, we can clearly see how external events and realities may have made such an impact on the child. They may too have severely impinged on what we would expect to be conditions for the normal development of a child. For children 'in transition' this will almost always have been the case. As child psychotherapists we are working constantly at the *interface* of the child's internal and external worlds.

Our psychoanalytically-based training starts from learning to *observe* infants and young children.[1] I would like now to present you with two contrasting pieces of observational material. I hope that these will help us to begin to focus on the difference in experiences and the capacity to reflect upon those experiences between a child growing up with greater continuity in a 'normal' family, whatever that is, and the precarious quality of the child 'in transition'.

Lily is aged 3½. She lives with her two parents and baby sister. On the afternoon of this observation the baby was asleep upstairs and Lily was playing on the floor with a pile of bricks and toy farm and zoo animals. Close by, her mother was sitting in a chair knitting.

> 'Lily sits on the floor arranging the animals, the cow and calf, the camel and baby camel, sheep and lambs, in a shed with the mothers and babies close to each other, looking at each other. She picks up the bull and looks at its genitals. She puts him down and then makes a separate house for him with some bricks. It is constructed with great care with a roof and chimney which she points out to her mother; but there is no door. She puts the bull in her house. She puts some fences together and puts the crocodile baby and mother together in the enclosure. On arranging the animals she has noticed that the kangaroo baby was not in the mother's pouch. She looks in the bag of animals for it and then she remembers where she put it last time she played with the animals. She finds it wrapped up in a piece of tissue with some other small animals and puts it in the mother kangaroo's pouch. She then places it in a field that she makes with some more bricks, together with some sheep. There are two parent sheep with a lamb in between them. She gets the toy pig sty and puts a mother and baby piglet in it. They are put together, very carefully arranged lying down. She says "they are suckling". She spends a very long time carefully putting the piglet's mouth to the mother's teat. She then sits and reflects for a while. She says she thinks they are just sleeping and not suckling. "They had a bad night last night". She looks back and checks that the piglet's mouth is actually resting on the teat. Then she tries, but fails, to fix a rubber band round the enclosure. She looks at the bull and says "to keep them safe".'

1 For a more detailed description of the training and practice of Child Psychotherapists see Trudy Klauber in *Rooted Sorrows* (Family Law, 1997).

Kerry is 5½ and lives with foster parents. The following is an extract from a psychotherapy session. Although I have omitted some of the interpretations which I as her therapist made to her, I have left in the description of my own feelings. The feelings that get stirred up in me can be thought of as powerful projections, communications of Kerry's own feelings and state of mind. As a child psychotherapist, one makes full use of these non-verbal communications both in understanding the child and in deciding what words to use when speaking to the child to help him or her find and develop his or her own sense of things.

> 'She rushes into the room and goes straight to her box and she tips up the small truck that is in it so that all the animals in it fall out. She notices that the kangaroo mother has no baby in its pouch. "Where is it?" she asks in a somewhat panicky way. She does not wait for an answer, nor does she seem to go on looking, but she rushes to the sink and turns on the hot tap (I feel anxious about what might have happened to the baby kangaroo. Has it even got lost in her last session and I did not notice? I am also thinking about her as a small girl who has so many things in her life that she feels she loses touch with, without understanding why. At the same time I can't see if the plug is in the sink and the water continues to rush in. However, I stay where I am and I am left with the anxiety of the possible overflow of the sink. As so often with Kerry I feel now that I am experiencing a whirlwind, like an overflow all over the place of her feelings, which have just been waiting for her arrival at the session.) Kerry leaves the taps on (continuing anxiety for me) while she comes back to the box and starts to take out the animals in what seems to be quite a random way. She finds the baby lamb and puts it into the kangaroo's pouch. She then asks me "Where is it?" I speak to her and she calms down a bit and I help her to see the baby kangaroo in the box of toys. She picks it up and rushes to the sink and flings it into the water. I ask what has happened and she tells me "it drowned". I speak to her describing what I see is happening and while I speak Kerry scoops up the baby kangaroo in the cup which is beside the sink. The cup is turned over and she tells me "it's a prison". She then quickly tips it out of its prison and back into the water again and seems to forget about it. I link what seems to be happening at the sink with her experience of separation from me. As I speak she beckons me over to the sink to have a look at what she wants me to see. She has turned the taps off and sink is quite full. Some animals are bobbing around in the water and some are at the bottom of the sink under the water. She pulls out the plug and then quickly puts it back in again. To my horror I see that the baby kangaroo is now under the plug and I am left with the terrible worry of whether it will go down the plug hole and be lost for ever. When she later pulls out the plug and lets all the water drain away I am enormously relieved that it is still there. Then I talk to her as I have done earlier about the danger to the baby and the need for it to be kept in mind so that it will not get lost and be swept down the plug hole. In the same way as she needs to know that I am able to keep her in my mind and be thinking about her during the week between our sessions. At this point she places the baby kangaroo in the mother's pouch.'

I think the really precarious quality of Kerry's play and the anxiety come across quite forcefully in this extract, as they did to me at the time. Nothing is experienced as given or as certain to be held onto; what cannot be seen may be lost forever. For Lily, on the other hand, there is time to remember where she has left the baby kangaroo and an expectation that she will find it. There is too the assumption of the gaze between the mothers and babies. The importance of gaze between mothers and babies is something that has frequently been brought to our attention both by child development psychologists and by reports of infant observations (Brazelton, 1991; Miller, 1989). In this brief piece of observational material of Lily we also see that she too has areas of anxiety. For example she separates the crocodiles from the other animals; how carefully she provides for the bull, who could disrupt the peaceful harmony of the mothers and babies. But at the same time this extract shows a continuity in her experience – she *knows* she will find the baby kangaroo.

Kerry is the child I wish to pursue in this paper as her experiences illustrate themes that are common to many of the children 'in transition' I have worked with or have heard about in the Adoption and Fostering workshop.

KERRY'S HISTORY

Kerry is a child of mixed racial parentage. Kerry has never met her Afro-Caribbean father. He mother who is white comes from Scotland. When Kerry was born she was just 16 and in Care. She had been heavily involved in drugs, alcohol and prostitution. Kerry's birth was normal and she and her mother spent her first six months together in a mother and baby home, apparently reasonably satisfactorily. However, after a row with a staff member her mother left the home suddenly. Kerry was placed with a foster family and remained there until she was three. Her mother kept in erratic contact with her for a while and then did not visit her for over a year. She reappeared unexpectedly, but Kerry pushed her away when she told her she was her mum. Her maternal grandmother had also established some contact with her, but stopped visiting at all for a while when she became worried that she herself would suffer if she was not allowed to see Kerry later on in her life.

The first foster placement ended when the foster mother committed suicide. She had involved Kerry in setting up the scene for the suicide.

Kerry's next placement involved physical neglect and ended after just over a year when Kerry and another foster child made allegations of physical abuse. After a brief bridging placement Kerry moved to her present foster family and has now been with them for two years. Mr and Mrs P are Afro-Caribbean. They have three children of their own, younger than Kerry. They are now asking for her to move to a permanent home. But they do not wish her to have to move unless the next home stands a good chance of being permanent.

LEGAL ARRANGEMENTS AND CARE PLAN

At her birth late in 1990 Kerry was made a Ward of Court and later her name was placed on the Child Protection Register. In 1993 she became subject to a Care Order under section 31 of the Children Act 1989. A guardian ad litem has represented her welfare and interests in court, most recently when the local authority made an application to end her mother's contact. At the same time, Kerry's grandmother made an application to become a carer for Kerry.

The most recent Care Plan was made two years ago when Kerry was 4½ at the time that she was placed with her present foster carers. It had then been decided that rehabilitation was not an option for her. The Care Plan was that she be placed in foster care until an adoptive home could be found for her. Shortly afterwards the court decided that Kerry should have no further contact with her mother. Arrangements for the frequency of contact between Kerry and her grandmother were to be at the discretion of the local authority.

Nine months elapsed between the endorsement by the court of this plan and the start of permanent family finding.

Kerry is a child who was Warded at birth, has been in Care all her life, has had four foster placements, in two of which she has been emotionally or physically abused. She is now 6½. Research shows that the earlier a child is placed for adoption the greater the chances of success. Breakdown rates for children who are older at the time of placement vary between 10% and 50%, increasing with the rise in the age of the child at the time of placement. Not surprisingly, breakdown rates are high when children have had early experiences of abuse within the birth family or care placements.[1]

When I read Kerry's Care Plan I was struck by how little was in it: it consisted of minimal phrases which could amount to all or nothing in terms of the planning for her life. Separate reports had provided more detail about her; but there was nothing in the Care Plan to link that plan to Kerry's needs. Moreover, could the decision about adoption have been made before she was 4½? Had it been, the chances of a successful adoptive placement would have been higher. The guardian ad litem had made an important contribution to planning. But there had been no input by a mental health professional even though there were already indications that Kerry's learning difficulties could be emotionally linked.

I am interested that the Health Advisory Service report *Together We Stand* (1995) on the commissioning role and management of Child and Adolescent Mental Health Services refers to the importance of the clinician's contributions to what it names 'Care Packages' for children and families. It backs joint planning for children, in the spirit of the Children Act 1989, in which the Child and Adolescent Mental Health Team, *having assessed a child's needs*, will augment local authority thinking with clinically driven 'care packages'. The intentions are there; but joint action at an early enough stage for a child so often seem to be very hard to achieve unless the child is demonstrating acute distress or behavioural difficulties. The *Review of NHS Psychotherapy Services in England* (NHS Executive 1996 para 3.10.14.2) looks at the question of the provision of psychotherapy and treatments for looked after children who are in difficulties.

> 'Careful planning of a treatment programme in an inter-agency context is usually essential to ensure that it is relevant, acceptable to all concerned, can be sustained and supported and is unlikely to be disrupted. Therapy is unlikely to alleviate a child's confusion and uncertainty if the latter is based upon the failure to agree a "Care Plan". However a child may value support during periods of uncertainty.'

---

1 For a review of some of the literature see David Howe 1997.

Incidentally, there was no mention in Kerry's Care Plan that she might benefit from psychotherapeutic help. When it was provided, there was inter-agency support. In her case there was less divide than there may be for many children between a carefully made Care Plan on the one hand, and an actual experience of lack of care on the other.

REFERRAL TO THE CLINIC

Kerry was referred for psychotherapy by her social worker from an outer London borough early in 1996. Her behaviour at that time was giving cause for great concern. With her foster parents she was rude and aggressive and was wetting the bed several times each night. At school she had become increasingly aggressive, seeming to hurt children and adults deliberately. All her behaviour had become more extreme when during the summer she was told that an adoptive home had been found for her. Although she had then been with her foster carers for only a few months she appeared, in spite of the succession of previous moves of care, to have become quickly attached to this new family and particularly to the children. Kerry's increased difficulties at this time were one of the reasons that the adoptive placement was not proceeded with.

Initially, consultations were offered by the clinic social worker and child psychiatrist to the professional network and to the foster parents. The child psychiatrist later wrote a report to the court on Kerry's needs and welfare, with recommendations for her future placement and contact with both mother and grandmother. I was asked to assess Kerry for psychotherapy.

THE ASSESSMENT

Kerry arrived with her gentle and very committed social worker for the first of her three assessment sessions. She was eager to come with me to my room, and, when she got there, immediately was disappointed that I did not give her chocolate to eat and only had little toys and not the 'big' ones she had hoped for. I found myself wondering if she, like so many children in her position had, at some level an expectation or thought that I might be going to be he new mummy. Once I had talked about her disappointment she looked to see what else might be available for her, but she did this in an angry and destructive and finally rather dismissive way. A week later she started the session angrily throwing a soft ball at me. I caught and ball and held it. I described what I was learning about her feelings in terms of the ball: although she threw it *at* me and had told me I was silly because I did not know about her sister's birthday, she could see that I was holding onto the ball while I was thinking about these things. 'Come on throw it at me.' I replied 'No, I will not throw it *at* you but I will throw it *to* you.' I lobbed it gently back to her and she caught it. She was delighted and a gentle game of catch began which lasted for a while until she became a bit excited. She finished up flinging the ball – miraculously it was held in the folds of the curtain. Now both of us were amazed and delighted. Kerry then started to move and explore the possibilities contained in the room and the toys. She showed she could think about all these things with me in a much more creative and thoughtful way than she had at the beginning of the session. This really seemed to offer some hope that she would make use of a psychotherapeutic setting.

What I have described is a condensed example of what Wilfred Bion described as a model for development for the infant and for the beginning of thinking: the infant who is still too immature to have the apparatus for complex thinking is thus unable to process his experiences in the world or within himself. By the intensity of his cry, for example, he projects his fear into his mother or carer. She feels his feeling, and by holding onto it, turning it over in her mind, or as Bion would say bringing to bear a quality of 'reverie', she processes the feelings. By feeding the baby, or by picking him up and holding him, or by struggling to understand what her distress might be about she detoxifies the intensity of the initial cry, the feeling of the infant. In her care of him she provides him as well with an experience of a mind, mediating the raw experience of the infant by her capacity to think thoughts. Over time and with enough of such experiences the infant is able to 'introject' and identify with a positive aspect of his care such that it becomes his own – he has taken into himself and acquired a space within himself for thinking thoughts. And thus he can find hope in making sense of his experience, both internal and external, for himself.

A large number of the children we see who have been unable to remain in their own families may not have had enough of such experiences. Indeed, this can of course apply equally to children who do remain in their own families. The children move through a world of persecuting experience, not just internally by having only a limited capacity to process and learn from their own experience, but too often compounded by adverse external experiences such as abuse or frequent changes of caretaker. Then, not thinking can become a defence against experience, particularly if the actual experiences are ones that it would be hard for anyone to comprehend.

So I was really delighted that Kerry showed that she could make use of containment to develop her own thinking and to move with some hope to explore what could be available for her. It suggests that she must have had a measure of good care, perhaps in the early days when her mother felt she herself was being held in the mother and baby home; also in her first foster home; and in the quality of thoughtful care she was receiving in her present foster home, which my social worker colleague was assessing.

This is the reason I chose to write about Kerry. She is not one of the children who seem to have no hope of making further attachments, or who seem to expect that they will never find a place, even in the therapist's mind, where they may one day belong. Nor is she one of the children who seem to attach too quickly, in an undiscriminating way, just dumping all the baggage of their experience on the therapist, and moving in.

However, there are still issues about whether or not to offer treatment to a child like Kerry. Received thought is that the child has to be settled, permanently placed, before therapeutic treatment can start. But the problem for the clinician with children like Kerry, who have already been on their journey for years and may be for still more to come, is what happens if she is left. She was already showing very disturbed behaviour at home and at school. She could be viewed as unadoptable. Kerry showed in the assessment how she can think about herself and her world, how she still wants to attach and find a secure home for herself both in fact and in someone's mind. This, in my view, is not the point at which to leave her to harden her range of damaging behaviours and defences.

Increasingly, children in Kerry's position are being offered therapy There has to be uncertainty about how long it will be available or may be jeopardised by further moves. But uncertainty is the name of the game for children 'in transition'. It is the currency of the therapy from the start. Margaret Hunter (1993) analysing a group of children in Care that she had worked with found that the average length of treatment she was able to offer was over one-and-a-half years. A year can be a long period in the lives of some of these children. But as we hear in the Adoption and Fostering workshop work with these children is usually extremely painful for child and therapist alike. Each case requires a lot of time around it. Not only do we have to think about our techniques of working with these children, we also may have to be in touch with a wide network of people who are crucially involved with each child. Kerry, for example, lived with her foster family, went to primary school and attended a special educational unit. She had a social worker who spent time with her fortnightly. The social worker had a manager. There was a social worker involved in family finding. A respite care worker took her on outings each week. Her grandmother saw her regularly. There was a guardian ad litem. There were regular reviews and professionals' and planning meetings, some of which Kerry knew about. What sense can Kerry make of such a network? It is not untypical. Indeed, she is fortunate because she has had fewer changes of a key social worker than many children who have been in care as long as she has. The psychotherapist has to make decisions about how involved to be in this wider world of the child. By tradition the psychotherapist works exclusively with the child and his internal world, and a social worker colleague engages with the network. We now often find that it is more in the *child's interest* that the therapist becomes more actively involved in discussions with other professionals. We must negotiate this interface in our work with the child in question. Interestingly, the children seem most often glad that their therapists do become involved in collaborative decision making for them. There are of course important questions about confidentiality which must be respected. For children 'in transition' tend to be very used to having less privacy around important aspects of their lives than most other children.

It was an agreed decision that Kerry should come for once weekly psychotherapy. Her foster mother was relieved. Social services agreed to provide transport to bring her to her sessions. The foster mother would also have regular sessions for herself with the clinic social worker. She told me that she asked Kerry why she liked coming to her sessions so much. Was it because of the toys or because she could do what she liked when she was with me? 'I like the talking' she stoutly replied. I was able to tell Mrs P how much Kerry gained from the talking with her too.

THE WORK WITH KERRY

The precarious quality that I spoke of in my first description of Kerry has been a continuing feature of the psychotherapy. It has been there in dangerous ways – the too hot water in the tap, the narrow window ledge, the attractive but dangerously tippy dest chair – horribly filled with associations to the suicide of Kerry's first foster mother. The sudden shifts in her feelings during sessions can lead Kerry to great anxiety about what it is in her that seems to drive people away – me, after a missed session, or foster mother whom she fears may leave her with me and drive off home in the taxi. She seems to wonder whether she, like some of the toys, will sink or float in the water in the sink. Most recently she has shown that she can feel like actually drowning herself in the water. She wonders whether I will be there to rescue her and prevent this happening.

Kerry's anxieties have been particularly keen at times of separation. It really is a question of whether I would be there, attentive enough in my mind but actually close enough as well. On one occasion I was not close enough and she fell off the desk where she was standing and hurt herself quite badly. But Kerry has been able at the same time to anticipate and think about holiday breaks, unlike many children including those in more favourable situations. In July 1996 she said, 'You are going on holiday'. She then smashed a polyfoam beaker with an effective karate chop. She climbed up onto the desk and stood up. With a rather far away look she said to me, 'I had a dream'.

> 'There was a big spider in a web and it needed help to get out. There were lots of baby spiders in the web. I killed the baby spiders and the spider ate them. It was in another web. A big yellow thing came and smashed my foot off but then the foot came back on again.'

A wonderfully rich dream. The interpretation of it developed through the rest of the session as we thought about her angry feelings about the babies she thought I would be busy conceiving and paying attention to during the holiday, and about the other children whom I might see in the therapy room. Her fears of retaliation for her aggression and her feelings about these things could also be thought about, at one moment very concretely because the blind she had damaged the previous week had been polished off by another child and had had to be removed from the room. Now she threw the soft ball *at* me again. Again I managed to catch it and hold on to it.

I want to focus on the detail of the impact on Kerry of knowing what she does not know and then of learning that she will be moving from her present foster home.

There had been a preview when the guardian ad litem had told her that she might not be seeing her grandmother again. In the event the court decided that the grandmother would continue to have contact with Kerry at the local authority's discretion. Kerry did not at first tell anyone what the guardian had said to her. But she started to wet her bed again many times each night (the wetting had never completely stopped) and she urinated angrily in her bedroom until the carpet had to be removed it was so saturated. She became more aggressive at school.

Early in 1997 at a professionals' meeting a more active plan for moving Kerry to a permanent adoptive home was developed. The foster parents, although they really love Kerry, find her very demanding. It is difficult for them to support the needs of their own growing family when Kerry's needs always seem to have to be attended to first. They pressed for permanent placement for Kerry, but said at the same time they will always wish to maintain their relationship with her. It was agreed that she would be told about the move after the summer, which carries associations to previous moves.

However, during the spring Kerry's behaviour began once more to become more difficult. At home she several times placed herself at real risk, and then repeated the dangerous activities. In two sessions with me she arrived angrily saying, 'Where is it? Where is my Barbie doll?' She seemed to think that I was wilfully hiding from her something that was hers. She was right. I was. I had information about her that I was not sharing with her. Here is one of the technical dilemmas for the therapist. Bound by an agreement with the other professionals I could not tell her of the actual move to come. A move I dread for her. But she seemed to know that something was afoot. However, while she is not told what that something is, she really cannot make sense of it. All the while her behaviour was deteriorating to the consternation of all who cared for her. So what do I say to her at this point? I tell her how angry I think she is with me because she thinks I am hiding from her something that is hers, something which she ought to have. She agrees with me but she still wants to know where the Barbie doll is and she is firm in her belief that I have given it to one of the other children I see. In fact she has never brought an actual Barbie doll to a session.

The next week one of her foster sisters is ill, then the following week Kerry herself is ill. After that for two weeks running the taxi failed to arrive to bring her to her session. Her foster mother rails against social services but is in fact beside herself about Kerry's behaviour. She wants her to have her sessions. 'She really needs to come. A little girl of her age should not have to think about the things that she has to think about.' Then I was on holiday over Easter and had to attend a clinic event on my first week back. So it was seven long weeks before I could see Kerry again. How precarious her whole existence is. Even what is set up to be reliable turns out not to be.

On her return her foster mother told me how the previous night Kerry was sitting cross-legged on her bed, not sleeping (she has previously told me about the 'buzzing' thoughts in her head that prevent her sleeping). She asked what she was thinking about because she knows that when Kerry sits in this position it means there is something on her mind. Eventually she said angrily, 'I want to go home, home, home'. Her foster mother told her that she was at home with them. With some difficulty Kerry told her that her social worker had said she was to go to a new home. In fact the social worker had not said anything to her. The point is that at some level Kerry knew that something was up and had struggled on her own to puzzle out what it was. Kerry had held this thought to herself all this time – just as she had previously with the information from the guardian about her grandmother.

When she saw me coming to collect her from the waiting room she gave me a dazzling smile. Arriving in the therapy room she was very quiet. She built a wonderful castle with bricks with a road leading to it broken by speed bumps – the exact number of the missed sessions. She communicated feelings of immense sadness, which became increasingly despairing as all the animals who thought they had a home in the castle were pushed out by a fierce crocodile. The crocodile could be thought of as representing her angry feelings, which are so often expressed in her urinating and destructive attacks which she feels then destroy all the better possibilities for her. The animals were dumped in a corner. We talked together about her anger with me for not protecting the sessions. Now too I could begin to talk about the real move that does lie ahead. Her sadness, despair and rage grew during the session. Kerry wanted to take away, to steal in effect from herself, the toys from the room, just as she has felt that I have stolen her Barbie doll. Now that she feels more persecuted her language is about stealing and not about hiding. She really feels her good home is being stolen from her but also she feels that she has destroyed it with her anger and with the strength of her needs.

I do not yet know if the new family will be a real possibility or whether Kerry has again been given premature information about an adoption that will abort as did the previous possibility two years ago.

FUTURE WORK

What can I, with my social work colleague, now do that could contribute to a hoped-for successful outcome of permanence for Kerry?

For a start we have a rather detailed picture of the child. We have seen how she can feel contained in a thoughtful 'talking' environment; how containment helps her actively to continue to be thoughtful herself, to wonder about her experience with another person, and to have hope still that there can go on being another such person available for her. However, we do also know that her very capacity for thoughtfulness makes her vulnerable. She can feel overwhelmed by her feelings and then can seek flight into behaviours which her carers may not be able to tolerate and which may place her at actual risk. My colleague can confirm from her work with Mrs P the qualities of thoughtful containment – love – that she has given Kerry. She also has evidence of how when things have been going well enough Kerry has been able to share that love with the three children of the foster family. There are still many things to feel hopeful about for Kerry. But this child 'in transition' is facing a major upheaval and change in her whole living. She is at her most vulnerable now. How much continuity can be maintained for her – with grandmother, or foster family, or school, or therapy – so that Kerry will keep hold of a feeling of the continuity of her own being, without which none of us can survive? We saw how continuity of being and of experience was such a resource for Lily to call upon.

It is important to consider what the prospect of moving from the family to which she is attached and where she has felt a strong degree of security will do to Kerry's future capacity to attach, and thus to the prospects for a successful placement. Sadly she is already showing that she is beginning to detach herself from her foster family. Her punishing behaviour is now making it more difficult for the family to maintain their attachment to her. The question remains: how many times can a child be expected to attach and to attach again? Especially when previous experiences have taught her that nothing is forever. Yet the phrase so often in current use about adoption is to refer to the 'forever' family. Is it surprising that some of these children 'in transition' can appear hardened and untouchable in their cynicism?

REFERENCES

Boston, Mary and Szur, Rolene (eds) (1983) *Psychotherapy with Severely Deprived Children.*
Brazelton, T Berry and Cramer, Bertrand G (1991) *The Earliest Relationship* (London: Karnac).

Hopkins, Juliet (1990) 'The Observed Infant of Attachment Theory' in *British Journal of Psychotherapy*, vol 6, no 4.

Howe, David (1997) 'Parent Reported Problems in 211 Adopted Children: Some Risk and Protective Factors' in *Journal of Child Physchology and Psychiatry*, vol 38, no 4.

Hunter, Margaret (1993) 'The Emotional Needs of Children in Care – an Overview' *Association for Child Psychology and Psychiatry Review and Newsletter*, vol 15, no 5.

Klauber, Trudy (1997) 'Child Psychotherapy: What is it? Who does it? How can it be useful?' in The Hon Mr Justice Wall (ed) *Rooted Sorrows* (Family Law, 1997).

Miller, Lisa; Rustin, Margaret; Rustin, Michael; Shuttleworth, Judy (eds) (1989) *Closely Observed Infants* (London: Duckworth).

NHS Executive (1996) 'NHS Psychotherapy Services in England'. *Review of Strategic Policy.*

O'Shaughnessy, Edna (1981) 'W. R. Bion's Theory of Thinking and New Techniques in Child Analysis' in Bott Spillius, Elizabeth (ed) (1988) *Melanie Klein Toady* (London: Routledge).

THIRD SESSION

PLANNING FOR CHILDREN'S SERVICES

Peter Kemp and Steven Ford

SUMMARY OF PAPER

Peter Kemp

Peter Kemp explained that as a Director of Social Services he was concerned with macro-planning. He noted that the public were often ambivalent about the role of social services as a 'corporate parent'. This was perhaps not surprising when one looked at the real problems and failures that had occurred for children in care in the past. He noted the recent political imperative to focus more on the development of preventive services for children rather than the more narrow focus on child protection; this inevitably had an impact on resource allocation (see Appendix 1 to this paper).

He stressed the need for aggregated data on outcomes for children to assist in service planning – to ask why outcomes were not being achieved. Mr Kemp also emphasised that the Children's Service Plans should be used to hold social services accountable for what they do and the partnerships they forge with others; the Plan should be a performance tool with measurable outcomes.

In the context of greater partnerships at all levels, including involving the children themselves, it was noted that this was a long-term programme aimed at promoting health, safety and protection, personal development and independence into adulthood. This new approach was not simply a matter for social services; the aims of such plans went across a wide range of disciplines.

Steven Ford

As a practising social worker, he focused on the practical application of care planning and accepted that the State often falls below the standard expected of 'good parenting'. He cited research by the National Children's Bureau (Appendix 2 to this paper) *showing the worrying failure of children in care. This highlighted the need to concentrate attention on outcomes. He suggested that part of the reason for such poor outcomes could be poor or unfocused care plans. The new 'Assessing Outcomes' approach was more holistic and far more prescriptive than previous practice. Whilst some social workers might find this difficult he felt that the evidence of the State's poor parenting in the past pointed up the need for such a new approach.*

Finally, he reminded the conference that making applications for care orders was a daunting prospect for most social workers and he highlighted the tension between professionals in what was often a very adversarial environment. He felt this often left the social worker feeling devalued and demoralised and he saw a need to develop greater partnership both before and during court proceedings to reduce the feeling of 'winning or losing'.

INTRODUCTION

The public perception which characterises the expected role of social services departments in working with children is largely governed by a view of the services dealing with residual children. Our planning for children is often seen to be aimed at controlling, or managing, behaviour in ways which will either protect the child or protect the public; children 'in care', in trouble, or in need of protection are seen to be our main targets. Our work in the family court can often be seen as adversarial with a local authority asking the court to intervene at a point of crisis because we have failed to deal with those matters ourselves through negotiation and mediation.

Whilst these views may, in some part, be true, they fail to take into account the painstaking work which social workers and others undertake to avoid crises and to promote the welfare of the child. The work that local authorities undertake under Part III of the Children Act 1989 in relation to children in need, including those with disabilities, mental health problems, runaways and young carers often escape public attention, but it is increasingly the case that our traditional focus on the individual child is being complemented by a requirement to plan more effectively for disadvantaged children living in our communities.

In March 1996 the Secretary of State for Health made an order under section 17(4) of the Children Act 1989 requiring local authorities:

- to assess the need for provision in their area of services under Part III of the Children Act;
- to consult with various bodies in planning how that need will be met;
- to publish the resulting plan.

Although Local Authority Circular (92) 18 had recommended that Children's Services Plans should be drawn up and had offered guidance on their content, the introduction of a mandatory requirement indicates the importance that the Department of Health attached to properly planned children's services. Local authorities were required to produce their first mandatory Children's Services Plan on 1 April 1997; as yet there has been no feedback on the quality of these plans from the Department of Health.

At the same time as the Government put pressure on local authorities to look at children's planning from a wider perspective, the Department of Health was developing a structured approach towards individual care planning for children in the 'looked after' system which is commonly known as 'Looking After Children – Assessing Outcomes'. This work arose from public concern highlighted by a number of high profile public enquiries during the 1980s that in some instances children cared for by local authorities were not protected from harm, and that children looked after were not experiencing outcomes their peers living in the community took for granted. By the end of this financial year 85% of local authorities in England and Wales will have adopted the 'Looking After Children' materials which should improve the quality of individual care planning. Aggregated information from individual Care Plans should reveal deficiencies in the systems which surround children in the Looked After System which mitigate against the achievement of the outcomes identified in the planning process. This should inform the effective development of Children Service's Plans to ensure that strategically such gaps are filled thus enhancing the life chances of children in the Looked After System. The question yet to be answered is whether or not the planning process adopted within the Looked After System is transferable to planning arrangements for children in the community; given that the planning system is based on outcomes for children there is a good chance that this will be possible. If Assessing Outcomes is about structuring social work intervention towards a parenting model, it has the potential to improve planning and its subsequent actions and consequences – for all children in contact with the local authority.

One of the enduring images of social services departments is their investment in child protection work. However, whilst the number of child deaths in England from abuse has halved over the last ten years, and the British record on child protection is second only in Europe to the Scandinavian protection system, the public image of the performance of social services departments is dictated by tragedies rather than successes. In 1993 the Department of Health published *Messages from Research* which looked at a whole range of research projects relating to children's services. That report concluded that whilst social services departments were very effective at the initial investigation and management of child protection, far too many of our resources were invested in this process. Far fewer resources were invested in family support to try and avoid child abuse occurring and reoccurring and in helping abused children to overcome the traumas they had experienced. The Department of Health's 're-focusing' initiative to encourage local authorities to shift resources from the initial investigation and management of child abuse to more family support orientated work was a welcome recognition of the significance of prevention; however, without additional resources, the penalties associated with moving money from child protection to family support are clear if, as a result of such re-focusing, local authorities are no longer able effectively to protect children.

Whilst this 're-focusing' debate has concentrated on the shift of resources from crisis work to prevention there is a view within some local authorities that social services departments have a key role to play in acting as a catalyst in bringing agencies around the table to address the universal needs of children and to assert the rights of children at a time when adults appear to de-value children's contribution, exclude them from decisions about matters likely to affect their future and in many other ways hinder their development as contributing citizens. For most of the time the majority of children are properly cared for by their families and make use of services available to all children in their local communities – for their health, their safety, their education and their leisure and recreation. The task facing statutory and voluntary agencies is to ensure that individually and collectively they provide relevant and coordinated services which value and support children and their families and which are committed to reducing disadvantage and discrimination. Negative images of the world within which young people operate, characterised by offending behaviour, irresponsible youth culture with its relaxed attitudes towards drugs, alcohol and social morals, run the risk of creating stereotypical responses by adults towards children with the attendant danger of reinforcing the prevailing sense of hopelessness felt by many young people. This process will further alienate them from the adult world.

Whilst the judiciary is rightly concerned about the future of individual children and young people and may justifiably be critical about poor planning by professionals, these individual outcomes may not just reflect the quality of individual planning but the culture and attitudes of communities within which these children and young people reside with their families. Tackling the agenda identified in the last few paragraphs is a significant component in developing positive attitudes towards children and their futures.

Running through this paper are recurrent themes which are essential in the planning process for children whether such planning is at an individual or collective level:

- partnerships;
- shared values;
- children's rights;
- children's participation;
- shared views about positive outcomes.

LOOKING AFTER CHILDREN – ASSESSING OUTCOMES

During the 1970s the interest in research into children in care increased considerably. Many studies highlighted deficiencies in the services then provided by local authorities. In taking on board feedback from these studies various strategies such as early prevention or permanency planning were developed but largely failed due to lack of evidence about the factors which might influence the development of children 'in care'.

In 1980, Roy Parker in his book, *Caring for Separated Children*, posed the question 'can the State parent?' As if in answer to that question, *Social Work Decisions in Child Care* published by the then DHSS in 1985 identified the isolation of children and young people in residential homes, their loss of contact with parents and their extended family and the general exclusion of parents from issues affecting their children whilst in residential care. Issues focusing on cost effectiveness and the targeting of resources began to emerge and a review of child care law was launched which resulted in the Children Act 1989.

In 1991, a working party, chaired by Professor Roy Parker, produced the report *Looking after Children: Assessing Outcomes in Child Care* (HMSO, 1991). This book developed the concept of outcomes and ways of assessing them in different contexts and focused on the concept of good parenting and its likely benefits. The study was unusual in that it linked the abstract concept of outcomes to professional social work practice; by using research knowledge it developed instruments that could be used to assess children's needs and follow their progress. The working party designed methods of monitoring children's progress at regular intervals so that plans for improvement could be added into the assessment process. Progress would be evaluated on the basis of the child's overall development. These assessment instruments record in one set of documents all the information needed to ensure a high standard of care. The Assessment and Action records assume a link between input and outcome and assess not only how far children are progressing along developmental dimensions but also the extent to which they are given the opportunity to succeed. Assessing Outcomes is, in short, about providing agencies/the State with the tools required to parent.

During the development stage of the project the Assessment and Action Records were piloted in five local authorities who between them completed assessments on a sample of 200 children in care or accommodated. At the same time they were also used to assess a randomly selected group of 400 children who were *not* looked after by social services departments. This research found that the Assessment and Action Records reflected the range of agreed aims of most parents in the community.

The key findings of this research were that children and young people looked after suffered a greater degree of isolation and instability than their peers living with parents; they had lower self-esteem and were less confident. Those children and young people looked after missed out on many aspects of their personal and social development. Children and young people who experience multiple placements are likely to underachieve at school and are likely to lose contact with family and friends. Those hobbies and skills which can create social opportunities and improve self-confidence are often foregone. Many of these problems will affect their adult lives, particularly the area of health which can be neglected in the care system.

Many local authorities in England and Wales have now adopted the 'Looking after Children: Assessing Outcomes' methodology and documentation. For those authorities who have reviewed use of the materials two significant themes emerge:

(1) the extent to which an outcome-based planning process empowers foster carers and residential social workers to act on behalf of children as a result of having clearer responsibilities for achieving outcomes;
(2) the much more significant contribution that children now make to plans about their own futures.

The local authority has a much better chance of acting as a good parent if members of the council can relate to outcomes for children in care in the same way they can relate to desired outcomes for their own children. The introduction of this planning process has, however, exposed practice shortfalls across a range of agencies and facing up to these difficulties has been a painful process and one that can lead to resistance and defensiveness on the part of individuals and organisations.

One of the most frequent and consistent criticisms of local authorities is the fragmented way in which they plan for children; changes in social workers, disrupted placements and other factors, have all contributed to this view. The systematic way in which material is recorded about children during their episode of care with the local authority should provide a thread of continuity capable at least of counteracting the impact of some of these disruptions. Equally, the reason why placements break down is very often to do with the failure of departments to work collaboratively with children so that they have a sense of their future and are committed to action. The Assessing Outcomes approach can improve this situation and provides a shared agenda between child/young person and their carers which may be capable of sustaining a placement on a more continuous basis.

One of the outstanding issues, of course, is that once the use of these materials has been pioneered in working with children in the looked after system, can they be adapted and developed to create a planning tool for children in the community who may experience levels of deprivation, disruption, disenchantment, conflict with adults, which in some cases could be the equivalent experience of a child in the looked after system? The transferability of these methods and skills could lead to improvements in the quality and continuity of plans for children in contact with family courts and youth courts.

CHILDREN'S SERVICES PLANS

Local authorities are required to produce an annual Children's Services Plan which demonstrates their response to a range of children's needs in their communities. The stated aim of a Children's Services Plan, articulated in the guidance documents published in March 1996 is to 'deliver better services to children'. The guidance identifies the United Nations Convention on the Rights of the Child ratified by the UK Government in 1991 and the Citizen's Charter as underpinning documents, and heavily stresses the need to develop procedures to talk directly to children and young people and to allow and encourage complaints and representations by young people about the services available to them. The order made by the Secretary of State requires local authorities to consult with:

- Health authorities;
- NHS trusts;
- Local Education Authorities;
- Governing bodies of grant-maintained schools;
- Voluntary organisations;
- The police;
- The probation service.

Significantly, the guidance recognises that whilst the new statutory requirement relates only to services for children in need, local authorities may want to consult and to plan more widely so that the result is a template for *all services for all children in the area.* The order advises that 'local authorities may wish to look at children in terms of the "whole child" and consider other services – such as transport, housing, leisure and environment which impact on their lives and help a child reach his or her full potential'. One of the issues to arise from the initial round of Children's Services Planning is the extent to which social services departments are best placed to produce the Children's Services Plan given this more 'holistic approach' towards the needs of children. The Conservative Government produced a White Paper 'Social Services: Achievement and Challenge' in March 1997 which stated in section 3.9,

> 'If the maximum effect is to be achieved, however, the planning process must be seen as the corporate responsibility of the local authority as a whole and fully involve other statutory services including Health, Education, Probation, other Juvenile Justice Services and Housing. The Government therefore proposes to widen the statutory framework accordingly.'

It is to be hoped that this element at least of the White Paper will be preserved and carried forward by the current Government.

The guidance on Children's Services Plans makes it clear that the first attempts of local authorities should address process issues in achieving the plan as a priority even if at the expense of explicit plans for children in their localities. This recognises quite rightly the interdependency of statutory and voluntary agencies in providing a comprehensive response to the needs of children and the extent of the work likely to be required to establish firm consultative mechanisms and partnership arrangements to ensure a cost-effective response to those needs. The significance for the family courts of the Children's Services Plan is that it identifies a comprehensive response by the local authority in relation to significant groups of children in our communities. At the very least the plan must cover:

- serices for children with disabilities;
- services for children and young people with mental health problems;
- services for children aged under 8 (day care);
- services for looked after children;
- young runaways;
- adoption;
- services for young people leaving care;
- family support for children in need and child protection;
- young carers;
- services for children and young people in conflict with the law.

It should be expected that a judge in the family court division wrestling with a particularly difficult case, in which the local authority was party to the proceedings, should enquire into what services and provision the local authority had made to address the issues faced by the court. In the final analysis, local authorities must be held accountable within the context of a mandatory Children's Services Plan.

It is equally significant that services for children in the looked after system are included in the Children's Services Plan as this cross-references with the individual planning processes outlined in the previous section. It is important that aggregated information from individual care plans inform the assessment of service/resource deficiencies in the Children's Services Plan. All too often social services staff have blamed the disruption of Care Plans on the pathology of the individual child rather than looking at the extent to which the environment within which a child lives and operates may have worked against the achievement of agreed outcomes for that child. For example, if individual Care Plans based on desirable outcomes for children identify a continuing trend towards the exclusion of children from school, professionals must be mature enough to assess the extent to which the school environment and regime have contributed to that exclusion rather than solely the individual attitudes of the student.

INVESTING IN CHILDREN

The invitation contained in the guidance on Children's Services Plans for local authorities to look at children in terms of the 'whole child' and to consider other services which impact on their lives, and help the child reach his or her full potential, has encouraged a number of local authorities to respond to the universal needs of children. In most local authority areas children aged under 18 make up nearly one-quarter of their population; however, because of their perceived immaturity and the attitudes of many adults around them, they have little or no voice in matters affecting them. There is a growing recognition that any failure to engage children and young people in decisions affecting them and to provide access to information on issues affecting their lives, will hinder their development as contributing citizens and as the next generation of parents. The task facing local authorities in this venture is in identifying the common ground between statutory and voluntary agencies in such a way as to reinforce the contributions of those agencies in dealing with the needs of children. For example, the planning officer within a local authority may not recognise his or her responsibilities for child protection but would recognise a responsibility for promoting the safety of children through improved road safety, safe play areas on new housing estates, better street lighting and environmental protection. Identifying these 'lowest common denominators' can create a consensus around the significance of a wide range of children's needs.

In seeking to underpin their activities through adherence to a set of principles and values most local authorities have turned to the United Nations Convention on the Rights of the Child which came into force on 15 January 1992, one month after it had been formally ratified by the former Conservative Government. The three underlying principles relate to:

- non discrimination (Article 2);
- the 'best interests of the child' (Article 3.1);
- the right of children to express a view on any matter concerning them (Article 12).

Whilst it is attractive to adopt the principles of the Convention for the purposes of uniting agencies in a common cause, the failure of government to meet the provisions of the Convention can generate scepticism within organisations about the local use of the Convention. In 1994 the Children's Rights Development Unit published the UK Agenda for Children which documented in detail how in almost every area of children's lives there is a denial of their basic rights to participation, protection and provision. The report was endorsed by more than 180 major national organisations and demonstrated breaches of the Convention in relation to personal freedom, physical and personal integrity, the right to adequate standards of living, health and health care services, rights in relation to youth justice, child labour and abduction. Government legislation and guidance drawn up since 1992 has largely ignored the convention, eg the Child Support Act 1991, the Education Act 1993 and the Criminal Justice and Public Order Act 1994 in relation to secure training centres. In *Health of the Nation*, the previous government's founding NHS document, there is no recognition of inequalities in health or children's rights.

Despite these difficulties, substantial progress has been made in developing a strategic framework which will both encourage local approaches to the involvement of children in planning and delivering services and the creation of a strategic investment programme which can make more efficient use of existing resources and gain commitment from a range of agencies to the planning and delivery of effective services for and with children.

The experience of some local authorities who are well down this road is that this broad approach must be seen as a long-term commitment. The culture change which is required to shift the balance of power in planning and decision making from adults towards children is enormous and adult perceptions of its benefits are slow to mature. Young children and young people who are members of school councils or elected to young people's organisations representing children's issues on local authority committees are rapidly enthused only to find the entrenched attitudes of adults difficult to overcome and in danger of reinforcing traditional stereotypes of adult/child relationships. The importance of listening to children and taking their views into account when decisions are being made cannot be over-emphasised. For children caught up in family breakdowns, bullying at school, peer group pressure on issues as diverse as offending, drugs and antisocial behaviour, the confidence to express a view rather than become a passive victim of circumstances is critical in developing a sense of worth and purpose.

THE CHALLENGE

The problem for social services departments in attempting to mobilise the resources and energies of other organisations to contribute to improvements in the quality of life for children as a preventive/social regeneration measure is that the majority of their resources are targeted on those most in need at an individual level. Despite attempts to break away from our narrow focus on children looked after, in trouble or in need of protection, we have at best begun to re-focus on children in need in our communities as required of us under the terms of the Children's Services Plan and the Department of Health's re-focusing agenda on family support rather than child protection. As a result the resources we have available to develop a wider investment strategy for children and young people who may not be the traditional targets of social services departments are extremely limited. In the same way that we rely upon partnerships with parents and professionals in individual care planning at the micro planning level, we must also rely on partnerships with other organisations at the macro planning level in order to make an impact in our communities. Without this longer-term investment in social regeneration and the creation of opportunities for children and young people to influence the evolving society in which they will soon be adults, the opportunity to build a social infrastructure which will value its young people, give them a sense of hope and maximise their life chances will be lost. Such failure will only reinforce stereotypical views by children of the adult world, a reality which will be characterised by the continuation of the current crisis management approach to services for children. There appears to be a growing recognition of the need to involve children and young people in decisions that affect them as part of a drive to improve concepts of citizenship and community. The timing is therefore right for multi-agency initiatives aimed at addressing the holistic needs of children as individuals and as a significant group in the population.

APPENDIX 1

Planning for the effective use of resources

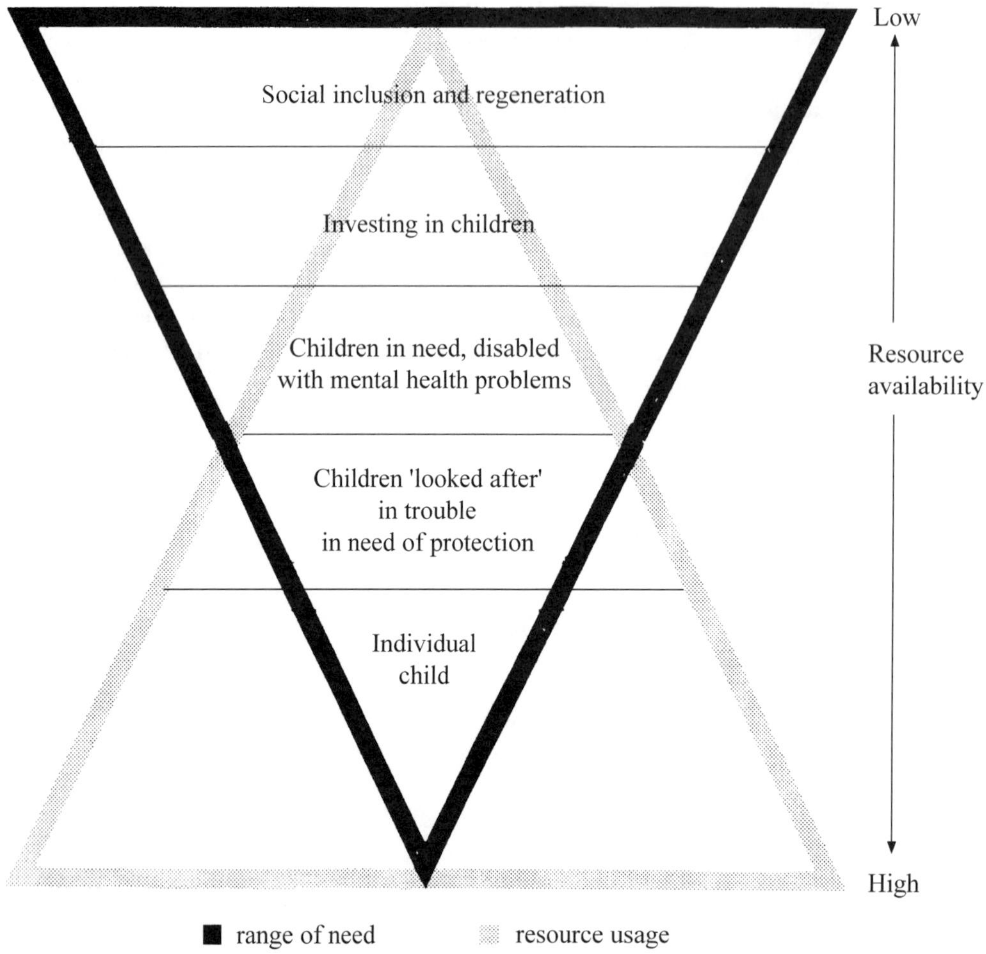

APPENDIX 2

Visible outcomes for 1995 National Children's Bureau

- Approximately 10,000 young people leave care each year.
- 75 per cent leave with no qualification, compared to 11 per cent nationally.
- 3 per cent get 5 GCSE passes compared to 64 per cent nationally.
- 0.4 per cent (1 in 250) qualify from a college or university, compared to 44.7 per cent of their non-care peers.
- 80 per cent of ex-care 18 to 24-year-olds are jobless, compared to 16 per cent nationally.
- 55 per cent of single homeless people have experienced care.
- 60 per cent suffer from serious health issues.
- 80 per cent experience destitution.
- 38 per cent of the young prison population (18–25) have experienced care.
- 22 per cent identify themselves as experiencing abuse.

FOURTH SESSION

RECENT RESEARCH IN CHILD WELFARE: IMPLICATIONS FOR POLICY AND PRACTICE

Professor Olive Stevenson

SUMMARY OF PAPER

In introducing her paper Professor Stevenson stressed the importance of research as laying the foundation for the principles underlying care plans. She expressed concern that there was a tendency to take an 'ahistorical' approach to research in care planning – one should not lose the importance of the older research in favour of trends. She welcomed the huge amount of research funded by the Department of Health, although thought that it would be regrettable if a situation arose where no funding was available for research save from the DoH. She suggested two questions arose in this field:

(1) What is in the child's best interests?
(2) What are the limits to that in practice when one has to take into consideration parents' rights?

The child's best interests

There was an enormous amount of research as to what consistutes good child development and most of this was now fairly uncontroversial. Her view was that it was in the practical application of the theory that there was much work to be done. She cited the example of lack of stimulation referred to in her paper – the implications of this had not been sufficiently examined. Similarly, the question of identity had profound implications for child placements and open adoptions and could be the 'death knell' for adoption as we now know it.

The impact of parents' rights

As to the importance of involving parents she stressed the need to learn sensitive ways of dealing with the principle of parental involvement as the process could be very painful indeed for many parents.

She suggested that there was broad acceptance of a principle that children were better placed at home where possible. The effect of this had been to create a profound public shift towards the idea of 'natural justice' for parents in, for example, cases of sexual abuse. Similarly, in the neglect cases where there was often much sympathy for parents doing their best and considerable work from professionals in an attempt to keep children with them if at all possible. The question of whether to keep children at home under a placement was also linked to the question of whether the system had anything better to offer such children. She felt more research was needed on the question of how to provide care for damaged adolescents and children. This was not simply a question of resources.

INTRODUCTION

I have been asked to give an overview of recent research in the field of child welfare. This is a formidable task, not simply because of the quantity available for review but because there needs to be an organising framework within which to set the research. Without this, the material would be disconnected and indigestible. However, the framework within which the research is presented has been determined by my own assessment of the most important contemporary issues in child welfare policy and practice and what appears to be those most salient to participants in this workshop. Inevitably, therefore, there is an element of subjectivity in the choices made and in the interpretation of the significance of results for policy and practice. Nor am I as familiar with some areas as others; delinquency is excluded for that reason.

As if that were not difficult enough, I have referred to some work which cannot be described as recent but which in my view should be used to underpin contemporary research. Present debates in child welfare lack a sense of history and this may make policy makers and practitioners vulnerable to swings and fashions which are not soundly based.

Although claims of research 'evidence' must be justified through references, there is growing irritation in academic circles at burdensome references, which may on occasion be more designed to impress than to illuminate. For this reason, I have not referenced assertions where they are very generally agreed or firmly established through extensive research.

The corpus of recent research on which this paper is based comes from a variety of sources. Obviously, it draws upon the work commissioned by the Department of Health under the title 'Studies in Child Protection' (HMSO, 1995) but there is other significant work which it is important to include, some also government sponsored but some independent, commissioned, for example, by the ESRC or by Charitable Trusts. There is no dispute that the Department of Health funding has been responsible for very important work. However, it is driven by particular policy priorities and there is little or no ability to fund spontaneous research proposals. The contribution of 'independent' research should not be overlooked.

PARENTS AND CHILDREN: DILEMMAS AND TENSIONS

Participants in this seminar will be painfully aware of the inherent difficulties in balancing children's needs and rights with those of parents. Even if the formal situation requires the child's interests to be put first, two difficulties remain:

(1) What is in the child's interests?
(2) What are the limits to that principle in practice when a parent's right to 'natural justice' is taken into account?

There are good reasons for assuming that some form of family life offers the best opportunities for the satisfactory nurturing and upbringing of children. We have a solid, extensive foundation of knowledge and research concerning children's developmental needs, intellectual, emotional and social and the conditions most likely to satisfy those needs. The fact that there are contested areas, theoretical disputes and, sometimes, difficulties in knowing how to apply particular research to important decisions about children's futures, should not blur some underlying certainties about needs which go beyond physical requirements for normal development. Three examples will suffice. One concerns *stimulation*, a child's need for appropriate cognitive and social stimulation (inseparable at an early age). The second concerns the need for attachment and bonding in early years to individual adults. This latter phenomenon has been the subject of intensive research over many years, and although the original work of Bowlby and others such as Rutter has been modified and challenged, the basic assumption holds good and remains a crucial factor in planning for children, especially when young. A third example, which has become clearer in recent years, both from research and from (painful) experience in child welfare practice, is that human beings have a profound need to develop a sense of identity through feeling 'connected' to their origins and roots (Bempah and Howitt, forthcoming). This is not simply to do with bonding/attachment to particular adults. It is now evident that the need goes deeper and further than that. It has led in recent years to hundreds, perhaps thousands, of adults sent by voluntary child care organisations to Australia and Canada as children, to seek out their families or origin; to a flood of enquiries to adoption agencies to trace birth parents and for some black or mixed race children a desperate wish to find parents who were black or to connect with their ethnic origins. Often to find siblings is of profound importance to such people. What then are the implications of such knowledge, confirmed by research and by experience? They are far reaching.

What of the need for stimulation? I use it as an example of an aspect of child abuse which has been alluded to as 'the neglect of neglect'. Neglect is one of the criteria used in the registration of children who are abused. Some of the constituents of 'neglect' are well recognised and uncontroversial, mainly those concerned with nutrition and hygiene. But the provision of 'good enough care' does not rest there; for example, failure to stimulate can lead to severe developmental delay (leaving children in cots or beds for long periods, failure to interact in play or conversation would be examples). There is research evidence that the long-term effects of persistent neglect may be more serious than sporadic physical abuse and the issue, linked to that of emotional abuse (Glaser and Lynch, forthcoming), is coming to the top of the child protection agenda. That is to say, health and social service professionals are increasingly aware of the importance of improving understanding and practice in cases of neglect in three ways:

(1) by widening the area of concern beyond the physical manifestations;
(2) by greater clarity about the *thresholds* for triggering concern; and
(3) by more effective intervention.

It is important that the role of the courts is taken into these considerations, in which what is regarded as significant evidence to establish neglect and some consensus about thresholds for intervention are critical factors. (My own work currently is on this subject, arising from ESRC funded research 1995 and, most recently, a Leverhulme Trust Fellowship to consider neglect from an interdisciplinary and interprofessional standpoint. [Stevenson 1996. See Appendix].)

Thus, a known and accepted developmental need, that of stimulation, has to be taken into the arena of child protection work. This requires sophisticated consideration of its implications for decision making.

The second and third examples, concerning attachment and identity, interlock in difficult ways. The traditional view of the importance of the former, led to prescriptions for placement policy, exemplified most clearly by the work of American lawyers and of psychoanalysts, (Goldstein, Freud and Solnit) in the 1970s, recently issued in one revised edition entitled *The Best Interests of the Child* (1996). The logic of that 'attachment' theory suggested that young children should have permanent placements at the earliest opportunity and that their needs for permanency should outweigh the wishes and hopes of natural parents to have them home 'in the future'. Their 'best interests' were seen as relatively clear cut. It has been claimed that, despite its US origins, these arguments had a profound influence on British placement policy in the 1980s. Certainly the phrase 'permanency placement' came into the policy makers' vocabulary at that time and led to suggestions that, after about 6 months in care, children should be found permanent substitute care. This drive was reinforced by research in the 1980s which found that children not discharged to their parents quickly were likely to remain in care for much longer periods (Millham, Bullock, Hosie and Haak (1986)).

But, whatever the policy makers suggested, the policy did not work, partly because it offended the field worker's sense of fairness and sympathy to struggling parents – which is later discussed.

In the context of this analysis, the emphasis on 'permanency placement' seems to conflict with the need to develop a sense of identity through connectedness to one's origins and birth family. The conventional model of adoption, for example, when doors closed on birth parents, is profoundly challenged by recent research and experience. In fact, the two areas of research are not irreconcilable if we can accept different models or patterns of upbringing. Whilst the security offered through relationships with certain stable adults is now seen as crucially important to young children, there is evidence (including that from other cultures) that they can and do make what may be described as secondary attachments to others. One of our difficulties lies in our cultural assumptions and the difficulties that this creates for adoptive and foster parents in accepting what may be described as 'inclusive' arrangements. None the less, it seems likely that greater 'openness' will increasingly be seen as crucial to help children (and the adults they become) make sense of their life history and origins. This has been widely accepted for children in residential care (the 'life story' book which they are helped to make is an example). Now it seems that this principle should be extended to those children permanently placed. Whether that means 'knowing about' or 'making contact with' will rarely be a clear-cut decision which can be taken once and for all. Nor would a general principle be rigidly applied to situations which vary hugely. But the basic assumption holds good.

Thus far, then, in addressing the 'child's best interests', I have stressed that there is a substantial amount of tested evidence concerning children's developmental needs, of which I have simply given three (albeit critical) examples and that these have direct bearing on policy and practice.

There is one additional point to be made to participants at this seminar, that is that whilst some delay in settling children's futures is inherent in tangled family relationships, the lengthy delays due to 'systems' and 'structures', including the judicial process, are impossible to excuse, when healthy development may depend on stable attachments made in early years. This was powerfully argued in the influential *In the Best Interests of the Child* in the 1970s. I do not know of evidence to show the situation has improved and there is current evidence in Britain of unacceptable delay, as in some child sexual abuse cases. The phrase 'abuse by the system designed to protect' is hard for professionals to hear, but it must be heard.

I have argued for 'openness' about families of origins and for doors in most cases to be left ajar, to be opened if and when it is desired to do so. This is not, however, an argument for contact or access in all cases. Decisions on that require complex and careful judgements concerning the value or harm to the child which may result from it, based on evidence of children's needs and their emotional state.

Although some of the foregoing discussion has concentrated on policy concerning children who do not live with their own parents, we can assume a consensus that strenuous efforts should be made to keep them with their parents (or with one parent) wherever possible. This has been part and parcel of an aspiration held by professionals and fostered by the legal process, that wherever possible, professionals should work 'in partnership' with parents, a term not mentioned in the Children Act 1989, but mentioned in the guidance. Such views were supported by ideologies, from the left and the right, of 'consumerism' and 'empowerment'. There has, however, been a danger that 'partnership with parents' could become a kind of slogan and that rhetoric could mask the reality, that there are inherent difficulties in such a concept. Fortunately, we now have some solid research on which to base the discussion.

One of the first tangible signs of the operation of the principle concerned parental participation in child protection case conferences. Policy at the Department of Health changed radically in the 1980s and reversed previous advice in the final version of *Working Together* (HMSO, 1988). This document suggested that it would usually be good practice for parents to attend such conferences. Obediently, most authorities initiated this with its attendant implications for practice and training. It was a neat issue for research and some significant evaluations were mounted which I have summarised and discussed (Stevenson, 1995). In general, those who undertook the work accepted the principle of participation, as being both ethically and practically desirable – likely to be the most effective way, wherever possible, of securing children's well being. Furthermore, some of the fears expressed by professionals, for example the dangers and difficulties of parental presence at case conferences, where found to be exaggerated and most professionals (not just social workers) found it to have been positive. Parents, in general, wanted to be there and valued the experience. However, a whole raft of emotional and practical difficulties were revealed by the research as needing attention if the practice was to be adequately developed and made rather less painful for parents. Painful it must always be; some of the 'user' accounts in the research show it to have been devastating for them. Following this, a much more extensive study of parental participation generally was carried out by Thoburn et al (1995).

In Thoburn's research, although the word 'partnership' is the starting point, she uses three dimensions, qualitatively different, 'participated', 'involved' and 'manipulated/placated' to measure parental activity in decision making. The research makes some carefully constructed assessments of these as viewed by the different participants, parents, children and professionals. The work is too dense and subtle to describe here but it shows that such research activity is well worthwhile in testing the validity of the overall objective, the extent to which it is being realised and the variations in perceptions of the participants about the process. (Some examples from this research will be brought to the seminar.) Most recently, there has been a developing interest in utilising the wider family network in the support of children and young people. This is exemplified in experiments with 'family group conferences' (a model originating from New Zealand) in which relatives and key people in children's lives are brought together to consider present difficulties and how these might be managed. Carefully evaluated projects have been undertaken; the findings of this research by Marsh and Crow will be published in the autumn of 1997 and show promising results, whilst not minimising difficulties and limitations. These projects demonstrate an attempt to give family members more power and responsibility and are thus consistent with notions of empowerment and partnership.

The reasonable assumption that working with parents, rather than for or against them, will benefit the child can fit quite comfortably with another, less explicit, concern about justice to, and sympathy towards, parents. In my view, the failure in Britain to implement a radical policy of 'permanency placement' was as much about this concern as it was about child welfare per se. This deep resistance to push the argument concerning the child's interest to extremes is illustrated by the reluctance of some professionals and some courts to admit 'defeat' in cases where they have struggled and failed to help parents improve their care of children, notably in cases of neglect where major, dramatic 'incidents' may not occur but in which children's lives are manifestly unsatisfactory.

A particular problem of our time concerns parents (often mothers) with learning disabilities who in a bygone age would have been prevented from caring for (or perhaps even from having) children. No one would now defend yesterday's practices but the necessary consequence of their bringing up their children is that difficulties in so doing will have to be addressed and that there will be times when the children's needs cannot be met within their own families. Evidence from inquiries and from research suggests that the nettle is not being grasped.

A further dimension of this identification with parents was seen in the wake of the Cleveland inquiry (1988), when powerful feelings concerning injustice to fathers were raised in the minds of the general public. Since that time, social workers (to quote a phrase from my ESRC research) have suffered from 'a sad sense of insufficiency', believing (with considerable justification) that there are children suffering and intimidated in their families where they are powerless to help. (I would welcome a discussion on this at the seminar.)

Two questions, therefore, must be posed. Can we, whatever the formal position, ever, in reality, relegate parental needs and rights to a 'lower division' of concern than those of children? Can we nonetheless refine our understanding of children's needs, and adapt our legal and organisational responses accordingly, to ensure better protection in their families for a wider range of disadvantaged and vulnerable children, not just those who sustain very obvious and observable trauma?

In making assumptions about the value of family life to children, I have so far avoided the awkward question, 'but what kind of family?' The radical changes in family structures and behaviour in post-war Britain are much discussed Most striking of all, with one in three marriages ending in divorce, with stable cohabitations and the forming of 're-constituted' families, society has been forced to re-examine long-held values and to face, head on, problematic issues concerning their impact on children. But there are other issues, though less common, which challenge us morally and emotionally even more. For example, questions concerning the upbringing of children within gay or lesbian households, the transracial placement of children, 'open' adoption in which children have ready access to a birth parent all raise intense feelings. The debate is often conducted without benefit of research evidence. To be fair, such research, involving as it does, longitudinal studies and evaluation of complex 'outcomes', is conceptually and methodologically difficult and expensive. At the time of preparing this paper, it has not been possible to evaluate adequately some very recently published work (and also to obtain findings of some research under way in the University of East Anglia on transracial placements). At the seminar, I will discuss in more detail currently available material.

What is clear, however, is that judgements increasingly have to be made concerning the welfare of children in what may be described (for how long?) as 'unorthodox' family arrangements. It becomes increasingly important that research on the effects of different family patterns on children should be developed.

THE ORGANISATIONAL CONTEXT

Studies in Child Protection (HMSO, 1995) has provided the basis for *Messages from Research* (HMSO, 1995), a document commissioned by the Department of Health and produced by the Dartington Social Research Unit. This is primarily intended for social services departments, it does not attempt to cover all the extensive implications and messages of these studies. However, this composite picture obtained of child protection policy and practice in recent years suggested that too many referrals were being subjected to what might be described as 'heavy' child protection procedures and too little work with families and children 'in need', as permitted by the Children Act 1989, was being undertaken. It was clear first, that to obtain services, children have usually to be defined as 'abused' and, secondly, that major improvements in assessment of child abuse had not led to effective strategies for intervention to support the families. This research has given a convincing picture of the organisational context within which child protection has been practised and, as such, can be mined for much valuable information, for example concerning the process of registration. Whilst much of this is not germane to this seminar, it is important to stress that we are now very well informed on 'how it works'. I suspect our research will be envied by academics and policy makers in other countries.

The findings of these studies have resulted in a sea change of policy at national and local levels. Child welfare services are in some turmoil. The policy 'steer' is clear. Much more should be done to offer service to children and families 'in need' whilst in no way reducing the quality of child protection against abuse. Social service managers and practitioners are ambivalent. On the one hand, such guidance is welcome because it fits with values and ideals about prevention. On the other hand, they cannot see how, at a time of such scarce resources, they can offer more to children in need and they are fearful about a backlash if abused children suffer. There is, however, some possibility of 'diversion', ie of helping some families and children without entering into expensive, labour intensive child protection activity. But it seems unlikely that much can be done by 'savings' in child protection to improve the service to needy families, of whom there are significant numbers. We are at a crucial juncture. It is of interest that this policy shift took place at the end of the Conservative administration and is in some ways out of line with the 'minimalist family intervention' suggested by their ideology.

CHILDREN AND YOUNG PEOPLE 'IN THE SYSTEM'

In contrast to the clear link between research and policy illustrated above, connections cannot be easily seen between research (using that term widely) and the provision of residential care for children. Long before the recent depressing revelations of past abuse, now widely discussed, there was solid research, from the 1950s onwards, which demonstrated first, that children in institutions, deprived of warm stable attachments suffered long-term damage and, secondly, that it is extremely difficult to provide what is needed within the existing structures and systems of residential care.

It is widely recognised that one of the reasons for the failure to offer sound, firm and sympathetic care to those in residential care was because the population changed, during the 1980s, predominantly to young people, rather than children; they were more difficult to 'manage' and the training for the staff was grossly inadequate. There will be much more to debate on this subject when the Department of Health publish another draft of research in 1998. For the purposes of this argument, I simply draw attention to the unrealised potential of such care for such youngsters when they and their families need a breathing space or when they need a refuge from abusive families. To have suitable provision of this kind is essential.

There is much further research to be done, including the use of evaluated projects, to see what contribution residential care can make to the spectrum of services available to children and young people. Although much research concerning residential care has not been effectively utilised, one initiative has been important and useful. This is the work known as the 'Looking after Children' project (Dartington Social Research Unit) in which very detailed guidelines for the assessment of the well-being of children and young people in residential care have been devised. Particularly valuable is the development of 'seven' dimensions of well-being: health; education; identity; family and social relationships; social presentation; emotional and behavioural development; and self-care skills. Each of these is assessed through carefully drawn questions. The value of it and difficulties in utilising it in practice are being carefully tested. The significance of this work goes beyond its use in residential care. It has considerable potential for working within families and may offer a helpful framework to the courts for the assessment of well-being of children in (amongst others) neglectful families.

Finally, a comment about the evidence from research concerning children's reactions and feelings to the child protection process in which they may become involved. Some excellent work has been done, notably that of Farmer and Oliver (1995) (a study of particular value in the HMSO series). The findings are of great concern (see Appendix) and show that at every stage of the process children suffer, are perplexed, ambivalent and anxious. If this is linked to the debate on legal procedures involving children, with which participants at this seminar will be more familiar than I, one has reluctantly to conclude that 'the system' may indeed be abusive, most particularly I suspect, in cases of sexual abuse.

CONCLUSION

This short paper does not do justice to the volume and quality of recent research. Nor does it address extremely important questions concerning methodology. These are not merely technical. The choice of method dictates what kinds of research questions can be asked. The paper does, however, identify certain critical issues in contemporary child welfare and suggests ways in which research has or could contribute to the debate on them. Broadly, there are four important strands of knowledge and theory, informed by research, which are crucial to the development of policy.

(1) *Child development* used to assess the well-being of children at home or in care and to identify adverse factors.
(2) *The organisational context*, including the courts, in which child welfare is practised.
(3) *The capacity of parents to develop and change* in caring for their children or to *fulfil their role* in unorthodox *family situations*.
(4) *The views and feelings of those* who take part in the process (parents, children, workers).

BIBLIOGRAPHY

Bempah, O and Howitt, D, 'Genealogical Correctness, Attachment Theory and Child Care Practice' in *Child and Family Social Work* (Blackwell, forthcoming 1998).

Cleveland 1998: Report of the inquiry into child abuse in Cleveland (HMSO).

Dartington Social Research Unit, 'Looking After Children' (various publications (HMSO, 1995)).

Department of Health, *Messages from Research* (HMSO, 1995).

Department of Health, *Studies in Child Protection* (HMSO, 1995).

Department of Health and Social Security, *Working Together* (HMSO, 1988).

Farmer, E and Owen, M, *Child Protection Practice: private risks and public remedies* (HMSO, 1995).

Glaser, D and Lynch, M, *Emotional Abuse* (HMSO, forthcoming).

Goldstein, J, Freud, A and Solmit, J, *The Best Interests of the Child* rev edn (NY and London: The Free Press).

Marsh, M and Crow, G, *Family Group Conferences in Child Welfare* (Oxford: Blackwell, forthcoming).

Millham, S, Bullock, R, Hosie, K and Haak, M, *Lost in Care* (Gower Press, 1986).

Stevenson, O, 'Case Conferences in Child Protection' in Wilson, K and James, A (eds) *The Child Protection Handbook* (Bailliere Tindall, 1995).

Stevenson, O, 'Emotional abuse and neglect: a time for reappraisal' *Child and Family Social Work 1996*, vol 1.1, pp 13–18.

Thoburn, J, Lewis, A and Shemmins, D, *Paternalism or Partnership? Family Involvement in the Child Protection Process* (HMSO, 1995).

FIFTH SESSION

CARE PLANNING: A DEPARTMENT OF HEALTH STUDY

Arran Poyser

SUMMARY OF PAPER

In introducing his paper Arran Poyser considered there were potential improvements to be made in care planning both before and after the making of any order.

A: Pre-order

There was much preparatory work which could be done before the making of the care order without in any way pre-empting the making of that order or pre-judging its outcome. An example occurs in cases where it is clear from a relatively early stage that the care plan is going to be for adoption. It was intended that good practice guidance should be issued to local authorities on this and on taking a pro-active role in similar situations such as freeing applications. He also noted that the proposed re-structuring of care plans set out in his paper did not contain any change in its composite elements; simply a new structure.

B: Post-care order

He took the view that any proposal to review care orders in certain cases needed careful and detailed consideration. The difficulty lay in the detail of how such a principle should work in practice. There were a number of possibilities to consider and he put forward some preliminary thoughts on how such a review process might work (see Appendix to this paper). *There were of course questions arising from such a proposal, such as:*

(a) What proportion of cases would be 'exceptional'?
(b) What are the costs implications and how are they justified?
(c) How should such a new system be monitored? How does one assess whether it is achieving what it was meant to achieve?

FIFTH SESSION

INTRODUCTION

Work was undertaken by the Social Services Inspector (SSI) in 1996 and 1997 which examined issues around care planning. The study – the latest in a series on the implementation of the Children Act is due to be published by the Department of Health later in 1997. Within this conference, I propose to deal with the following themes:

- how care planning developed within Department of Health policy;
- what local authority front line staff said about care plans made in the first six months of 1995;
- how a range of judiciary reported their experiences in using plans in proceedings;
- whether the care plan guidance issued by the Department of Health in 1991 is still helpful;
- whether involvement of the courts might improve practice and whether oversight of care plan implementation is a possibility in terms of revised policy.

I also need to refer and pay tribute to many others who have contributed to this area or are currently working on it. Joan Hunt's research from Bristol University funded by the Department of Health has resulted in a series of fascinating papers under the generic title 'Statutory Intervention in Child Protection'. The complete research is due to be published in a few months. Professor Judith Harwin from Sussex University is also being funded by the Department to look in depth at this topic and she will report in about two years' time.

Lastly, may I emphasise that as far as possible a clear distinction is made (and intended) between descriptions of official departmental policy and other ideas in this paper which are not official policy.

CHILDREN ACT AND GUIDANCE

Prior to the implementation of the Children Act in October 1991, in seeking a care order from the court there was no requirement that local authorities should set out their proposals for the child's fuutre. Of course, many did so as a matter of good practice. The new principle at section 1(5) restricted courts by directing that they should only make an order if doing so was better for the child than making no order. The 'no order principle' as it is frequently called, introduced a new stage into the court stage beyond the satisfaction of the threshold criteria of specific sections such as significant harm. Neither the Act nor subordinate legislation makes explicit reference to care plans. A section in the court application form for a care order (Form C13) requests a plan for the child or children and leaves a 7 cm gap to complete this.

Considerations about care planning are very much left to the guidance issued in 1991 by the Secretary of State. This developed an outline framework for planning the care of every child looked after by local authorities. It is used mainly for children who are accommodated who are the much larger group than those the subject of a care order. Currently there are something in the region of 5,600 orders made per year under section 31 of the Children Act (*source*: The Children Act Advisory Committee Final Report June 1997, p 76). At any one time there are about 49,000 children looked after by local authorities in England. Nevertheless, what was essentially a tool for internal local authority planning purposes took on an increasingly important function in court proceedings. Successive judgments stressed the significance of care plans and the duty of the court to scrutinise them. This 'adoption' by the courts of a list of issues which was never designed for courts has contributed to some of the difficulties and tensions experienced in this area – particularly in the triangle of local authority, court and guardian ad litem. Later in this paper I will offer a revised and, I believe, more logically ordered list for inclusion in the plan.

There is also another point of potential tension within this triangle and which sometimes seems to be based on a misunderstanding of the provisions within the Children Act. As far as courts are concerned, section 1(1) is well known: 'When a court determines any question with respect to the upbringing of a child ... the child's welfare shall be the court's paramount consideration'. A guardian ad litem could be said to act under a lower welfare standard. Section 41(1) states that '... the court shall appoint a guardian ad litem for the child concerned unless satisfied that it is not necessary to do so in order to safeguard his interest'. Does this imply that the guardian's welfare duty is to 'safeguard the child's welfare'? The Family Proceedings Rules 1991 are silent on the weight the guardian is to put on the welfare of the child. Certainly, the principle at section 1(2) (avoidance of delay) is explicitly mentioned at rule 4.11(1) which requires the guardian to 'have regard to the principle' and to the matters set out in section 1(3)(a) to (f) (the welfare check-list) 'as if for the word "court" in that section was substituted the words "guardian ad litem"'. But, as for putting the welfare of the child as the guardian's paramount consideration, this appears more a professional aspiration than a legal requirement and is reflected as such in the National Standards for the Guardian ad Litem and Reporting Officer Service (DoH/Welsh Office, 1995) which at Standard 4 states 'In each case under the Children Act the guardian ensures that the child is the paramount consideration; in adoption cases, the guardian safeguards the interests of the child'.

There is no doubt what the welfare standard is for local authorities. Section 22(3) states that it shall be the duty of a local authority looking after any child 'to safeguard and promote his welfare'. A large local authority, perhaps responsible for several hundred children being looked after, has an identical duty to each of them. It can of course prioritise and, in a practical sense, many need to do so in order to match needs and resources. But it cannot, unlike the court, be compelled legally to consider the child before the court in terms of paramount welfare.

It needs to be emphasised that planning has the positive purpose of safeguarding and promoting the child's welfare. The 1991 guidance explained that the drawing up of an individual plan for each child looked after would prevent drift and help focus work with the family and child. Such plans should constitute an essential element of the Arrangements for Placement of Children Regulations 1991 which cover all looked after children. Although the term used is 'arrangements', they are to all intents and purposes care plans. Regulation 4 requires the responsible authority 'to have regard so far as reasonably practical ... to the general considerations specified in Schedule 1, the considerations concerning the health of a child specified in Schedule 2 and the considerations concerning the education of the child specified in Schedule 3'. The contents of these respective schedules are as follows.

Schedule 1 – Considerations to which responsible authorities are to have regard

(1) In the case of a child who is in care, whether an application should be made to discharge the care order.
(2) Where the responsible authority is a local authority whether the authority should seek a change in the child's legal status.
(3) Arrangements for contact, and whether there is any need for changes in the arrangements in order to promote contact with the child's family and others so far as is consistent with his welfare.
(4) The responsible authority's immediate and long-term arrangements for the child, previous arrangements in respect of the child, and wether a change in those arrangements is needed and consideration of alternative courses of action.
(5) Where the responsible authority is a local authority, whether an independent visitor should be appointed if one has not already been appointed.
(6) Whether arrangements need to be made for the time when the child will no longer be looked after by the responsible authority.
(7) Whether plans need to be made to find a permanent substitute family for the child.

Schedule 2 – Health considerations to which responsible authorities are to have regard

(1) The child's state of health.
(2) The child's health history.
(3) The effect of the child's health and health history on his development.
(4) Existing arrangements for the child's medical and dental care and treatment and health and dental surveillance.
(5) The possible need for an appropriate course of action which should be identified to assist necessary change of such care, treatment or surveillance.
(6) The possible need for preventive measures, such as vaccination and immunisation, and screening for vision and hearing.

Schedule 3 – Educational considerations to which responsible authorities are to have regard

(1) The child's educational history.
(2) The need to achieve continuity in the child's education.
(3) The need to identify any educational need which the child may have and to take action to meet that need.
(4) The need to carry out any assessment in respect of any special educational need under the Education Act 1981 and meet any such needs identified in a statement of special educational needs made under section 7 of that Act.

The Arrangements for Placement Regulations 1991 also require arrangements concerning the matters specified in Schedule 4 to be included where practical. The contents of this Schedule include the following *but the regulation makes the important distinction of excepting a care case*. We therefore have a set of planning regulations which *excludes* material for care cases, only to have many of these items *included* via the requirements from the Court of Appeal. Such confusion is not helpful!

Schedule 4 – Matters to be included in arrangements to accommodate children who are not in care

(1) The type of accommodation to be provided and its address together with the name of any person who will be responsible for the child at that accommodation on behalf of the responsible authority.
(2) The details of any services to be provided for the child.
(3) The respective responsibilities of the responsible authority and:
  (a) the child;
  (b) any parent of his; and

(c) any person who is not a parent of his but who has parental responsibility for him.

(4) What delegation there has been by the persons referred to in paragraph 3(b) and (c) of this Schedule to the responsible authority of parental responsibility for the child's day-to-day care.

(5) The arrangements for involving those persons and the child in decision-making with respect to the child having regard to:

(a) the local authority's duty under sections 20(6) (involvement of children before provision of accommodation) and 23(3) to (5) of the Act (general duties of the local authority in relation to children looked after by them);

(b) the duty of the voluntary organisation under section 61(2) and (6) of the Act (duties of voluntary organisations); and

(c) the duty of the person carrying on a registered children's home under section 64(1) and (2) of the Act (welfare of children in registered children's homes).

(6) The arrangements for contact between the child and:

(a) his parents;

(b) any person who is not a parent of his but who has parental responsibility for him; and

(c) any relative, friend or other person connected with him and, if appropriate, the reasons why contact with any such person would not be reasonably practicable or would be inconsistent with the child's welfare.

(7) The arrangements for notifying changes in arrangements for contact to any of the persons referred to in paragraph 6.

(8) In the case of a child aged 16 or over whether section 20(11) (accommodation of a child of 16 or over despite parental opposition) applies.

(9) The expected duration of arrangements and the steps which should apply to bring the arrangements to an end, including arrangements for rehabilitation of the child with the person with whom he was living before the voluntary arrangements were made or some other suitable person, having regard in particular, in the case of a local authority looking after a child, to section 23(6) of the Act (duty to place children where practicable with parents etc) and paragraph 15 of Schedule 2 to the Act (maintenance of contact between child and family).

This paper does not set out to review all the key judgments relating to local authory care plans although some are available in the Appendix to this paper.

Local authority front line staff

The SSI study findings were based on work in four local authorities in the South of England selected by SSI. They are not named in the study. In the department's studies of the implementation of the Children Act, the identities of all authorities, courts, guardians and children are anonymised. Care plans made in the first six months of 1995 were examined – about 30 were the subject of this study.

What emerges from many of the cases examined are the following impressions:

- Social workers and social services departments are investing significant resources in maintaining children in their families of origin, often using other resources to assist.
- Balancing the risks of 'preventive' work with taking definite action to remove children continues to be problematic and such decisions appear to be taken only when any additional crisis triggers them.
- Health and education authorities may not always adopt the required total family view to sustain children at home, or provide assessment resources, or further resources for children in care.
- Neglect was significant in the cases of younger children coming into care.
- Drugs/alcohol were features in most of the cases.
- Mothers' mental health was a feature in a few of the cases.
- Cultural differences in child-rearing practice were claimed as an issue by the two refugee families in the study.
- Work with families of origin is done in a committed and sensitive way. Although the lack of contested orders in the final hearing indicates an acceptance of the plan, or passive resistance, at best there is evidence to show that workers were dedicated to informing, involving and supporting parents and were generally successful in this.

- Cultural, religious and racial considerations were taken very seriously, but the needs of young people from refugee backgrounds were not able to be met appropriately in all aspects of their lives.
- Relationships with colleagues in other departments, agencies and the GAL panel were generally viewed positively.
- Resources were seen as an issue in some instances either in obtaining appropriate and speedy specialist assessment and importantly in reducing appropriate family finding and placement. Most of those interviewed considered that resources were going to become increasingly problematic and one authority identified the method of managing the budgeting process itself as unhelpful in planning for some children/young people.
- In general, the care planning process is working. SSDs show a high level of commitment. Attempts are made to avoid drift through review meetings and there was evidence that these reviews are held regularly. In one authority a departmental chair manages this process. The legal department, however, has a key role in managing the court process and lawyers are often dissatisfied with the priority given to the detail of court work in preparing written and presentation material. Lawyers recognise the demands on the social worker but consider managers should provide more time for preparation, and themselves take more responsibility, relying less on legal colleagues.

JUDICIAL PERSPECTIVES

Interviews with judiciary were conducted with the help of a pre-circulated proforma. The interviews included family proceedings court chairs (stipendiary and lay magistrate), district judges, care centre judges and judges in the Family Division at the High Court. Interviews took place in London and the north of England.

All stressed the importance of the care plan, that it must be practical and reflect available resources. The plan needed to be a separate document and it was unhelpful if it rehearsed the local authority's case which was already addressed in evidence. The plan 'makes the local authority nail its colours to the mast'. The care plan also helped the court because it was difficult to understand the local authority process of planning and how they made a decision.

The main difficulty about care plans was that they were too short or too long. Plans were not always though out regarding the detail, might be too vague, and have no flexibility. Some were too hopeful when factors still had to be assessed – eg rehabilitation after assessment. A further difficulty was when the local authority changed its mind during the course of proceedings. This gave rise to distrust by other parties, particularly parents. Variations between local authorities could be marked. A format or framework could be helpful.

The main difficulty was the non-implementation of the plan. The court needed a responsible document. The plan might be there – 'we will do X' but it may lack details about the process and how the plan has been arrived at. Quality thinking may be missing. 'A plan which has clarity and transparency achieves credibility.'

Despite these perceived difficulties, the judicial interviews showed that the plans had generally improved in the last two years. There was greater awareness by local authorities of the relevant judgments. More often, care plans were more management-based indicating that the documents had been prepared by the head of the team rather than the case-worker. There have been physical changes, particularly regarding format. The Wall judgment has been followed by the majority of the local authorities. The Department of Health publication *Reporting to Court* (HMSO, 1996) has also helped, specifically addressing local authority care plans for court at chapter 14.

Judicial opinion differed on some issues such as the handling of siblings. Where the plan for siblings was the same, it was more helpful to have them all in one plan but if the children had different needs, it needed to be differentiated. Another view was a preference for a separate document for each sibling but with the additional comment on the effect on the other siblings of implementing the plan for each child. A third view was that there should be no separate plans for siblings and this avoided repetition. 'It is difficult in separate plans quickly to find the bits that *are* different.'

The judiciary were of one mind in respect of what courts looked for in a plan – an exploration of what is proposed, why it is proposed and the clarification of choice where necessary. There was also agreement that the status of the plan was not a formal promise nor an undertaking but 'a statement of joint intent, made in good faith'. Within these processes courts needed to be proactive, particularly at directions, in guiding or advising or questioning aspects of the care plan and progress in its preparation. Directions might include 'issue to be addressed'. One of the judicial interviewees said: 'remember, there is an important difference between a court asking that an issue be addressed and telling a local authority what to do'.

THE CARE PLAN FRAMEWORK

The Adoption Bill which was published as a consultative document in 1996 included a clause which dealt with care plans. This proposed a new subsection at section 31(3A) of the Children Act which said 'no care order may be made with respect of a child until the court has considered a plan for the future care of the child prepared under section 31A'. Section 31A made it mandatory for the local authority to prepare a care plan within a timetable set down by the court. It also required the local authority to keep the plan under review and, if some change was necessary, to revise it or make a new plan. The plan must give any prescribed information and do so in the prescribed manner.

That Bill has not yet been given Parliamentary space and it is not possible to say if or when this might happen. For the time being, it seems that care planning if it needs to be improved, must operate on a good practice consensus across the field rather than within an amended statutory framework.

The list itself of 18 items set out in the guidance and endorsed by the Court of Appeal is rather illogically presented.

(1) the child's identified needs (including needs arising from race, culture, religion or language, special educational or health needs);
(2) how those needs might be met;
(3) aim of plan and timescale;
(4) proposed placement (type and details);
(5) other services to be provided to child and or family either by the local authority or other agencies;
(6) arrangements for contact and reunification;
(7) support in the placement;
(8) likely duration of placement in the accommodation;
(9) contingency plan, if placement breaks down;
(10) arrangements for ending the placement (if made under voluntary arrangements);
(11) who is to be responsible for implementing the plan (specific tasks and overall plan);
(12) specific detail of the parents' role in day-to-day arrangements;
(13) the extent to which the wishes and views of the child, his parents and anyone else with a sufficient interest in the child (including representatives of other agencies) have been obtained and acted upon and the reasons supporting this or explanations of why wishes/views have been discounted;
(14) arrangements for input by parents, the child and others into the ongoing decision-making process;
(15) arrangements for notifying the responsible authority of disagreements or making representations;
(16) arrangements for health care (including consent to examination and treatment);
(17) arrangements for education; and
(18) dates of reviews.

This list jumps from issues to do with the child's needs to overall aims of placement; to who does what; to contingency arrangements; and to the role of parents. This no doubt reflects the hectic timetable in 1991 within which the volumes of Children Act guidance had to be prepared. I believe we now can do better. This paper therefore proposes that the plan should have five sections into which all but one of the 18 items can then be fitted. These are:

1 overall aims;
2 child's needs;
3 views of others;
4 placement details and timetable;
5 management and support by local authority.

Within these sections (the guidance order is numbered in parentheses) the list of 18 would look as follows:

Section (1) Overall aims	Aim of plan and time scale (3).
Section (2) Child's needs	The child's identified needs (including needs arising from race, culture, religion or language, special education or health needs) (1). The extent to which the wishes and views of the child have been obtained and acted upon and the reasons for supporting this or explanations of why wishes/views have been discounted (13). How those needs might be met (2).
Section (3) Views of others	The extent to which the wishes and views of the child's parents and anyone else with a sufficient interest in the child (including representatives of other agencies) have been obtained and acted upon and the reasons for supporting this or explanations of why wishes/views have been discounted (13).
Section (4) Placement details and timetable	Proposed placement (type and details) (4). Likely duration of placement in the accommodation (8). Arrangements for health care (including consent to examination and treatment) (16). Arrangements for education (17). Arrangements for contact and reunification (6). Other services to be provided to child (5). Support in placement (7). Specific details of the parents' role in day-to-day arrangements (12).
Section (5) Management and support by local authority	Who is to be responsible for implementing the plan (specific tasks and overall plan) (11). Dates of review (18). Contingency plan, if placement breaks down (7). Arrangements for input by parents, the child and others into the ongoing decision-making process (14). Arrangements for notifying the responsible authority of disagreements or making representations (15).

A few of the 18 items are split or partially repeated to separate out and give greater emphasis to the child's perspective (eg 13). One is not used at all as it applies to accommodated children and not to those in care (arrangements for ending the placement if made under voluntary arrangements (10)).

There are other practice improvements which could also be considered. These include the plan being signed by a senior local authority manager and a further separate section setting out what the financial estimates for implementing the plan might be. The latter idea is fraught with difficulties because there is currently no nationally agreed method of costing the different elements which might make up a typical care plan.

About 120 local authorities in England have adopted the Department of Health 'Looking After Children' assessment, review and action forms. Indeed, there has been gratifying interest from all round the world with many organisations obtaining licensed agreements to use the materials. Here the care plan comprises an eight-sided A4 proforma of some 27 principal questions. Those which correspond with the court care plan requirements are highlighted with a coloured symbol. Unless these documents are retained by social workers on computers, there is no straightforward way at the present time of avoiding some duplication of effort in respect of children who are accommodated and then become the subject of care proceedings. This could be addressed by the Department of Health in any revision/update following further monitoring of the general implementation of these materials.

However, whilst the needs of the courts are clearly crucial, there remains an important debate as to whether improvements in care planning should be in respect of all looked after children or if, instead, developments should specifically concentrate on those children the subject of care applications, with the consequent risk that the present system might evolve in two increasingly divergent directions.

CHANGES IN OVERSIGHT OF CARE PLAN IMPLEMENTATION

The curtailment of the use of wardship in 1991 was a specific change in the legislation brought in by section 100 of the Children Act. In general terms, many of the judiciary regretted this change and it has been a subject which has frequently been referred to. At its simplest, so the argument goes, the court should retain a reviewing power over the actions of local authorities when the latter are charged with implementing the care plan pursuant to a care order.

Before the Children Act 1989 many local authorities relied extensively on the wardship provisions. This is not the place to review the ranges of reasons which encouraged that practice. However, one category which was supported by a line of judicial thinking emphasised the advantages of sharing with courts certain exceptionally difficult decisions facing local authorities.[1] This had in more recent times led to discussions at conferences and in other settings about what may be termed 'Post-Care Order Court Review'.

This thinking seeks to bring some change to the present situation where, having made a care order, the court has no continuing involvement in or knowledge of the implementation of the care plan. The areas of discussion which need airing cover a range of practical and legal points. Of course, what is fundamental is whether the policy which lay behind section 100 and the decisive cut-off point at the making of a care order should in any way be disturbed. Before any change in policy were to be proposed, more detailed thinking is needed.

There are a number of questions which come to mind:

(i) What criteria might be used to target review cases either at the time the care order was made or subsequently by the parties?
(ii) What should be the functions of the review and the powers of the court?
(iii) What processes might facilitate such a review including possibly the need for further statements, an updated guardian's report etc?
(iv) What forum would be most suitable – a full court hearing or something more akin to an extended directions hearing?
(v) What are the financial implications for all concerned (including legal aid) and how might costs be justified and carefully contained?
(vi) What level of court should be able to exercise a review function?
(vii) How might the perceived benefits of such a system be best articulated?
(viii) What legal changes are necessary to bring about any desired change?

Some of these points were discussed in the spring of 1997 by a number of family division judges. That they favoured a post-care order review will come as no surprise. They considered that this might be

1 Lane J in *Re B (A Minor) (Wardship: Child in Care)* [1975] Fam 36, [1925] 2 WLR 302. Ormrod LJ in *Re Y (A Minor) (Child in Care: Access)* [1976] Fam 125, [1975] 3 WLR 342.

achieved by the local authority or the guardian having the power to refer the matter back before the court within 12 months of the making of the care order. As there was insufficient time on that occasion to discuss all the questions listed above, more detailed consideration was needed if a sufficiently robust case for legal change was to be made out.

Further discussion took place a few weeks later and this mapped out a possible procedure for a care plan review. At the same time, a number of considerations remained to be clarified. These included the 'exceptional test' of between 1% and 5% of cases to which any review might apply (ie perhaps under 200 care order cases per year); the potential costs of additional court time, legal representation, guardian and local authority costs; and mechanisms for monitoring any new review system. The suggestions arising from these discussions are summarised below.

1. **Threshold criteria**
   The review mechanism should only be activated in exceptional circumstances where:
   (a) the change in the detail in the plan is significantly contrary to the welfare of the child;
   (b) unforeseen circumstances make the care plan inappropriate;
   (c) the local authority is unable to implement the care plan as originally presented when the care order was made.

2. **Timetable**
   (a) a care plan review may be initiated in the period up to 12 months following the making of the care order;
   (b) application for leave for a care plan review hearing should be heard within 14 days of the application;
   (c) the application should be to the court which made the care order;
   If, however, the order was made in the family proceedings court, the application and any subsequent hearings should be at the appropriate care centre court (because of the difficulty of convening the same bench of magistrates that had heard the original care proceedings);
   (d) the review hearing should be timetabled within 4 weeks of the application for leave being granted.

3. **Bringing the application**
   The care plan review may be sought by the guardian ad litem or the local authority only. In most situations, it is expected that leave for a review will be sought jointly by the guardian and local authority. The parents will not have leave to apply for a review.

4. **Review power**
   The review power is limited to endorsing a new care plan.

5. **Repeat application**
   The care plan review may only be used once in the duration of any care order and only in the first 12 months of that order.

6. **Notifying the guardian**
   (a) appropriate legislation would require local authorities to send to the guardian ad litem copies of all case conference notes and/or review notes of each case conference and/or review following the making of a care order for a period of 12 months;
   (b) the guardian would review the documents only; if the guardian considered that it was necessary to apply for a care plan review hearing, the guardian would be required to discuss the proposed application with the local authority before making the application.

7. **Reports for review hearing**
   For the review hearing, the local authority would need to produce a new care plan detailing the specific changes. The guardian would be required to produce a supplementary report and undertake enquiries which include seeing the child and discussing the new plan with the local authority.

8. **Involving parents**
   Those holding parental responsibility would by notice be advised of the date of the care plan review hearing. They would be eligible to advice/legal aid and to attend.

9. **Other family proceedings applications**
   Legal provision would also be needed to prevent the care plan review being joined with any other application (eg an application to discharge the care order).

Other suggestions about improved practice have been made which do not involve changes to the legal framework. One such initiative being taken forward by the Department of Health and the Lord Chancellor's Department (LCD) is in respect of care plans and adoption. The Children Act Advisory Committee in its *Handbook of Best Practice in Children Act Cases* (June, 1997) again drew attention to the difficulties in the section on care plans (p 8):

> 'If the plan is for an adoptive placement, the court will be handicapped in assessing the plan and the timescale, unless the child concerned has already been considered and approved by the adoption and fostering panel, and potential suitable adoptive families have been identified. It is not good practice to await the making of a care order before obtaining such information, because the court is deprived of important background information and significant delay can occur in placing the child in the event of the court approving the plan.'

The Department plans a Chief Social Services Inspector letter to local authorities and voluntary adoption agencies setting out best practice in this area. Because expectations between courts and local authorities can be confused, a parallel guidance note to courts is being considered by LCD. Thus it is hoped that both local authorities and courts will not only be assisted in the steps leading up to the submission of the final care plan but also have available at the same time the complementary guidance note and therefore be more fully aware of mutual expectations and needs.

CONCLUDING COMMENTS

The material presented in this paper is essentially about improved practices by local authorities whilst at the same time questioning whether some of the fundamental responsibilities of court, local authorities and guardians ad litem might need to be re-aligned. There are issues about power and control – who has how much – and whether it is exercised in a way which promotes the welfare of children.

The good news is that the SSI study points to the court satisfaction with the quality of care plans generally presented by local authorities. Real improvements have occurred. Similarly, local authorities are clearer and more confident in delivering realistic plans which are appropriately succinct without missing out vital detail.

What we know less about are the reasons why care plans change. This is essentially for long-term research and, as mentioned earlier, work of this nature is being undertaken. Joan Hunt's invaluable study *The Best Laid Plans: Outcomes of Judicial Decisions in Child Protection Cases* will be published later in 1997. We have to assume in the absence of contrary evidence that most care plans are successfully implemented, albeit with sensible adjustments at certain moments in time to reflect the reality of a child's developing and changing needs. But a health warning is needed – a successfully implemented care plan should not be equated with a successful outcome of a happy and trouble-free child, adolescent or young adult.

Joan Hunt's research illustrates many of the problems faced by children on entering the care system rather than as a consequence of being in care. For example, in her research sample, by the final hearing in the care proceedings 48 children needed some permanent substitute care of whom for 27 the firm plan was adoption. But adoption was not a straightforward matter. Hunt reports that of these 27:

- eight children were aged 5 or above, one being 7 and another 10;
- 14 were members of sibling groups;
- four were of non-European parentage;
- 17 had particular educational, medical or other special needs;
- 24 had a parent suffering from psychiatric illness, learning disability or some form of addiction.

Hunt also comments that whilst each of these factors on their own might not significantly complicate the search for adopters all but four children fell into more than one of these groups, with six presenting potential difficulties in three areas, nine in four and three unfortunate children in all five. This is even before one adds in any effects of abuse or neglect, separation and public care.

Care orders are, by and large, only made in the most difficult and worrying of cases. Instant cures do not exist – for some children the best achievable outcome might be little more than the so-called 'damage limitation exercise'. Predicting what course of action will best promote the welfare of children remains hugely difficult for the courts themselves, but also for those in a professional and advisory role in the court proceedings. This is not an exact science and decision-making therefore needs to be approached with great care and, frankly, a substantial degree of humility. Sound assessment and planning can be of fundamental importance.

APPENDIX

Care Plan Review

Outline stages – threshold criteria

The review mechanism should only be activated in exceptional circumstances where:

(a) the change in detail in the plan is significantly contrary to the welfare of the child;
(b) unforeseen circumstances make the care plan inappropriate;
(c) the local authority is unable to implement the care plan as originally presented when the care order was made.

Timetable

(a) A care plan review may be initiated in the period up to 12 months following the making of the care order.
(b) Application for leave for a care plan review hearing should be heard within 14 days of the application.
(c) The application should be to the court which made the care order. If, however, the order was made in a family proceedings court the application and any subsequent hearings should be at the appropriate care centre court.
(d) The review hearing should be timetabled within 4 weeks of the application for leave being granted.

Who may bring review application?

The care plan review may be sought by the guardian ad litem or the local authority only. In most situations, it is expected that leave for a review will be sought jointly by the guardian and local authority. The parents will not have leave to apply for a review.

Review power

The review power is limited to endorsing a new care plan.

Repeat application

The care plan review may be used only once in the duration of any care order and only in the first 12 months of that order.

Notifying the guardian

(a) Appropriate legislation would require local authorities to send to the guardian ad litem all case conference notes and/or review minutes within 14 days of each case conference and/or review following the making of a care order for a period of 12 months.
(b) The guardian would review the documents only. If the guardian considered that it was necessary to apply for a care plan review hearing, the guardian would be required to discuss the proposed application with the local authority before making the said application.

Reports for review hearing

For the review hearing the local authority would need to produce a new care plan detailing the specific changes. The guardian would be required to produce a supplementary report and undertake enquiries which include seeing the child and discussing the new plan with the local authority.

Involving the parents

Those holding parental responsibility would by notice be advised of the date of the care plan review hearing. They would be eligible to advice/legal aid and to attend.

Other family proceedings applications

Legal provisions would be needed to prevent the care plan review being joined with any other application (eg application to discharge care order).

Other considerations still to be clarified

(a) The exceptional test suggests applicability to between 1% to 5% of care orders made per year (ie under 200 per year).
(b) Potential costs to be clarified include:
  – court time;
  – local authority;
  – guardian service;
  – legal representation for parent and child,
(c) mechanisms for monitoring any new system.

SIXTH SESSION

OVERVIEW OF DAY 1

Michael Leadbetter

SUMMING UP AND COMMENTS

It would be invidious to seek to summarise such a rich set of presentations. What I propose to do is to share aspects of the presentation which made a strong impact on me, both as a Director of Social Services, and a child care professional.

The Hon Mr Justice Wall and The Right Hon Lord Justice Thorpe made a very strong case for courts having more responsibility for monitoring Care Plans. In essence, this is an argument for monitoring how local authorities spend money.

This approach was broadly supported by psychiatrists and psychotherapists – not in a confrontational sense, but more out of a genuine sense of frustration where, at least from their perspective, Care Plans were not being properly followed. They were sometimes, it seemed, ignored or changed. Dr Claire Sturge said, in her view, 50% of the cases she had been dealing with had been unsatisfactory.

Jenny Kenrick reminded us of the pain and despair of the children we were discussing, with a very moving portrayal of 'Kerry' – commenting that the perceived thought is that children have to be settled permanently before therapeutic treatment can start. This is a chicken and egg dilemma for therapists and local authority workers. In my view the treatment needs to start as soon as possible. Our children cannot afford to wait. It may be less than perfect, but it is better than nothing.

Peter Kemp gave a very important reminder of the context in which the local authority social services children's services operate, sharing with us, in a very helpful way, a diagram that I am sure can happily be plagiarised for its clarity – and the fact that it was on one side of A4 (see Appendix 1 at p 44).

Professor Olive Stevenson reminded us of the importance of research, looking at how we balance children's needs and rights with those of parents, and confirming what most research says, that family life offers the best opportunities. Professor Stevenson identified three key areas:

(1) Stimulation.
(2) Attachment.
(3) Identity.

The other key point concerned the need for the courts to differentiate between appropriate delay in proceedings, which could be due to the tangled family relationships, and inappropriate delay, which was due to systems, structures, and judicial processes.

Arran Poyser, from the Department of Health, set out expectations of a Care Plan and shared some ideas for improving the quality of Care Plans.

My overall impression of the day is one of high-quality debate, both in the plenary sessions and in the groups, a strong commmitment from all parties to improving the welfare of children, and very proper discussions regarding roles and responsibilities.

This is my opportunity to share the local authority perspective.

Local authorities generally, and social service departments specifically, are the most inspected and externally audited of organisations.

We are subject to internal inspections from:

- County Treasurer's Audit Section;
- Chief Executive's Department reviewing functioning of the arm's length Inspection Unit.

Externally from:

- The Social Services Inspectorate;
- The Audit Commission;
- External Audit scrutiny linked to, but separate from, the Audit Commission;
- The Health Advisory Service;
- The Mental Health Act Commission;
- Scrutiny of cases by guardian ad litem;
- Regulation which gives Ministers wide-ranging powers to involve themselves in social services activities;
- The Ombudsman.

Yet here we propose, with I know the very best of motives, that guardians monitor cases for perhaps six to 12 months and that judges have the power to recall and review Care Plans.

I will pose the following questions.

If judges, and I believe this would need primary legislation, determine that they will review Care Plans and make orders in respect of the local authority, on what basis will they make these orders? How will they enforce them? What happens if the local authority is spent up? Judges do not interfere in determining medical priorities, why should they interfere in determining social welfare priorities?

Do we know the extent of the problem? In this I support the view expressed that we need to undertake some research. Claire Sturge says that 50% of the cases coming before her are of real concern. 50% of what? If it is 50% of a very small sample, it may be important for those children, but is that significant enough for wide-ranging changes in the system? If the average is 50% of a much larger sample, this is a cause of real concern.

I am not for one minute saying that social services departments always get it right. We do not. Some of our Care Plans are not of sufficient quality and we do need to recognise this, and take action. But what action?

Before moving on to make a proposal, I would like to deal wtih some myths.

There is, first, the myth that external inspection and monitoring helps solve problems and manage situations. It does not. There seems to be a growing belief, perhaps it has now reached its peak, that separation of function and imposing external inspection and review was a way of managing difficult issues – the Health Reforms are a case in point. In my view it is not. At best it is a safeguard, at worst it can be a smoke screen, and give false reassurance.

The other myth is that the more arm's length the inspection regulation and review is, the more effective its function. I would argue that this is not proven. Arm's length functions have their place, but there are inherent dangers of this kind of separation. Losing touch with professional expertise, lack of day-to-day contact with the problems, and, crucially, the separation of power and responsibility. My experience has taught me, time and time again, that when we separate out responsibility for delivering services from proper authority over those services, there is a disaster waiting to happen.

What then is the answer? In my view, it is relatively straightforward. Directors of Social Services are responsible for what occurs in their departments. They should be properly held accountable if Care Plans, in whatever forum, by the courts, the guardians, or indeed external inspection from the SSI, are deemed to be inadequate. There are mechanisms for holding directors accountable through the Social Services Committee and the Department of Health. I would have no objection to being written to by judges or guardians concerning the quality of a Care Plan. It is interesting that this seldom occurs, and often people who write to complain, write to the very staff who have carried out the faulty assessment in the first place. I imagine there are areas of complaint in the department regarding Care Plans, and yet I may not know about them.

Secondly, if there is a view that some kind of legislation and change is required, let us focus on the correct target. In Essex we have a monitoring and reviewing system for children's cases. This section of the department, which is managed by a senior manager, reports directly to the Head of Children's Services. The manager is untrammelled by operational responsibilities and given the task of ensuring that reviews (these include child protection case conferences) and Care Plans are properly assessed, formulated and presented. He is answerable to the Head of Child Care and, ultimately, to me, and has free access to the operational managers who are at exactly the same level in the organisation. If we want to look at requiring social service departments to do anything, why do we not require them all to set up similar independent (but within the child care system) reviewing structures? Then departments and directors could be properly held accountable, fudge could be eliminated, or at least dealt with appropriately.

What about guardians monitoring the Care Plan for six to 12 months?

Exactly the same reservations apply to guardians, as I have set out already, plus one more. If guardians undertake additional duties, it will cost money. In my view, it would be an unnecessary extra set of checks and balances. Unnecessary if departments are reviewing and monitoring their cases properly, perhaps along the lines set out previously. It would also cost money. There would bound to be extra costs involved. I also believe it may require a change in legislation because it is not part of the guardian's current role and function as laid down. As a Director of Social Services, if we are going to spend extra resources, I would like to spend the cash on social workers. It is, to say the least, illogical to consider spending extra resources on monitoring through the guardians, when those extra resources could fund social workers to deal with the unallocated cases which are a feature of so many social services departments.

To sum up, therefore, I do wish all the people involved in child care could have a sense of the intelligence, commitment and passion of this conference. The offer by psychiatrists and psychotherapists to work alongside staff in the social services department, to help them prepare plans and to assume their proper share of responsibility, is a wonderful offer made with grace and commmitment to children. The commitment of all the judges present to get the system right and put children at the centre of it is heart-warming.

My thanks to you all.

SEVENTH SESSION

GUARDIANS AND CARE PLANS: CUTTING THROUGH THE CONFLICT

Tess Duncan

SUMMARY OF PAPER

Having been a guardian ad litem since 1985, Tess Duncan introduced her paper by stating it was an attempt to look at some of the sources of conflict between guardians and local authorities and to try and present some alternative solutions to disputes other than the court process. She noted that most guardians come from a social work background and thus have the same professional background as a social worker but have a different role to play in court proceedings as an independent party. This in itself can create tensions between the two.

Review

She referred to a number of the examples in her paper and considered the question of what form of reviewing mechanism might be put in place to try and avoid the sort of difficulties which arose in those cases, particularly of drift.

She presented a proposal formulated by the guardians at the conference (see Appendix to this paper). *It was noted that this proposal had very real costs implications and the question of where the money would come from to fund this had to be addressed. However, the cost was perhaps relatively modest compared to the cost of caring for these children when the care plan has gone wrong and very expensive placements have to be used. She also stressed that she was proposing only a very limited role for the guardian in monitoring the care plan – perhaps limited in time to 12 months after the making of the care order.*

She also emphasised the need for good care planning before the making of the order as research suggested that those plans which had been subject to lengthy consideration and scrutiny at court were those which tended to have the best record of success.

She also noted the role for the guardian in addressing practice issues with the local authority such as that referred to in her paper on purchaser/provider problems and in contributing to Children's Service Plans. There was undoubtedly much to be achieved through greater communication between guardians and local authorities.

INTRODUCTION

What follows is informed by my own experience. I work as a manager of a guardian panel and as a guardian on a different panel. Like most guardians I was trained by and gained most of my experience in local authority social work, before becoming a guardian in 1985. I am not a lawyer so my use of case-law in this paper may not be authoritative.

Social workers and guardians have the same professional roots, yet frequently find themselves in conflict over care plans. I propose to look at some case examples in order to explore what lies behind this conflict, to identify the causes, and consider ways forward. I have gathered these examples from colleagues across the South East of England, as we share similar conflicts and dilemmas at regular meetings. They are not a statistically valid sample, but are reasonably representative of the type of conflicts which arise. In these examples I consider what other factors influence the local authority's decision-making, how this impacts on the care plan and what is presented to the court. Ultimately, it is the court which must decide whether the plan is satisfactory.

The guardian ad litem service was set up to provide the courts with independent social work investigation and advice. It was made a responsibility of local authorities (Panel Regulations 1983 and 1991) since they were the main providers of social work and thus the source of relevant expertise. I attach in the Appendix a breakdown of the work of the guardian service to illustrate the volume of that work. Being the responsibility of local authorities does impact on the need to be seen to be independent and does cause guardians some difficulty. This, combined with having the same professional background, means that guardians must ensure that they reach their conclusions on the best outcome for a child without the influences which may be constraining the social worker. They need to demonstrate their independence to the child, the child's family and the court.

Dame Margaret Booth (Booth, 1996, 11) highlights the tense and difficult relationship between guardians and social workers. Social workers often feel disadvantaged in court since they perceive the guardian's evidence as always preferred, while the social worker's is seen as of less value. Both groups, however, share the same professional background and often have comparable experience.

The panel manager, who is usually, like myself, employed by the local authority, is like a buffer between the independence of the guardians who are members of that panel, and the need to ensure some accountability and value for money for the local authority. The guardians themselves are accountable to the court which appointed them, for their recommendation. The social worker is, however, accountable to the local authority. The social worker's recommendation and care plan is the local authority's position. It may not always be that the social worker agrees with the local authority's position, which may be governed by resource constraint, the social worker's manager's view or the advice of the expert appointed by the local authority.

I acknowledge that there is room for improvement in the practice of some guardians and social workers, and this impacts on the quality of what is put before the court. I will be considering this from a guardian perspective.

EXAMPLES OF CONFLICTS OVER CARE PLANS

Conflict between guardian and local authority expert

Having experts involved in cases often causes problems over timetabling. In one case where the local authority expert was late filing her report (there had been an agreed letter of instruction) the timetable became concertinaed.

> The social worker and guardian had expected a recommendation of permanent removal of the children from the family, since the expert had expressed much concern about the harm the three children had suffered in their parents' care. They were aged 9, 3, and 2. This expert recommended a further attempt at rehabilitation. The local family centre had been working with the family for four years, and had much evidence of the high risk posed to these children in their parents' care. All parties were expecting a final hearing, but the guardian sought advice at short notice from another expert and decided that the care plan of rehabilitation posed too high a risk to these children. The guardian recommended a further interim care order to enable the court to remain involved to scrutinise the plan.
>
> This caused some consternation since it was seen as introducing further delay. The local authority response was to express concern that they were seen as needing such scrutiny, while the social worker privately told the guardian that he shared the concerns. An interim order was made after lengthy negotiations outside court, with the reluctant agreement of the local authority.
>
> In *Re T* [1994] 2 FLR 423 Nourse LJ clarifies that the court has a duty to scrutinise the care and contact plan of the local authority so as to satisfy itself that the plan will indeed promote the child's welfare. In this case the rehabilitation plan did not work and the case came back to the court three months later with a care plan for permanent removal of the two older children and a protection plan for the youngest. By this time the parents had accepted that they could not look after these children and were in agreement with the care order.
>
> Keeping the court involved meant that there was an external authority which acted as a catalyst to ensure a final agreement.
>
> In this case the social worker and guardian were not in conflict but the social worker's hands were tied by his authority accepting its expert's position.

Over-rigid application of local authority policy

Another example of conflict is where the guardian and the social worker may be in agreement but the social worker is restrained by his authority's policies.

> The need to control spending on social services is an influence on these policies. In one local authority a decision was made to control the amount of money spent on placing children outside the local authority's resources. This was understandable since £4 million was being spent annually on such placements and it was argued that this money could be

better spent on developing preventive services. A panel of senior managers was set up to consider all decisions about placing children outside the local authority. A guardian was involved in a case where both she and the social worker agreed that the eight-year-old child, who had suffered sexual and emotional abuse, needed a specialist placement outside the local authority. The first care plan stated this and named the resource. Before the final hearing, however, the panel turned down the case and the social worker's plan had to be changed. The plan now stated that the child would be placed in a children's home within that local authority. The guardian disagreed with this, as did the judge, who questioned the basis of the changed plan and refused to make a final order. The judge directed that the guardian visit the specialist placement and report back to the court as to whether it was the right placement for the child. The guardian concluded that it would meet the child's needs. The judge made it clear to the local authority that he would not make a care order unless the local authority reversed its second care plan and placed the child in the specialist placement. This was done and a care order made. This direction by the judge does not seem to me as a non-lawyer to fit with *Re J* [1994] 1 FLR 253 where Mr Justice Wall warned of 'the danger of using an interim order as a means of exercising the now defunct supervisory role of the court'. It did, however, result in the child being placed where the guardian felt his needs would be met. Court Rules do require the guardian to advise the court about 'any other matter concerning which the justices' clerk or the court seek his advice or concerning which he considers that the court should be informed' (FPC (CA 1989) R 1991, r 11(4); FPR 1991, r 4.11(4)). I pose the question: was this a legitimate interpretation of this rule?

One of the local authority's senior managers put in a complaint to the guardian's panel manager, questioning the competence of the guardian to assess the residential placement. There were strong feelings aroused about the guardian having the power to question local authority decisions about use of resources. The guardian informed the child's solicitor and he informed the judge about the complaint. The judge wrote to the Director of Social Services to ask for an explanation of this action. There was an investigation and the complaint was withdrawn.

In this case the conflict was between the guardian and the local authority, not the social worker, and is an example of conflict heightened by resource constraint.

Another example of this is where a local authority, faced with escalating costs of care cases, made a decision to 'gate-keep' all cases requiring care proceedings.

Social workers were required to justify decisions to take proceedings to senior managers on a 'diversion panel'. Social workers told guardians that they were advised against referring adolescents to this panel since they would be turned down because adolescents were seen as difficult and expensive to care for and experience suggested that intervention rarely produced a desired result. In one case involving a very disturbed 14-year-old boy, proceedings had started when this panel came into operation. When the case was referred, the panel ordered that the interim order made in s 37 proceedings should be allowed to lapse. The guardian, when informed of this, requested that the members of this panel give evidence to explain why this decision had been made. In the end a full care order was made with an agreed care plan for a residential placement. Delay and stress to the child, the family and the social worker was caused by what was felt to be a bureaucratic decision applying a blanket policy.

Social work practice

Guardians are more frequently being re-appointed in cases some time after care orders have been made. Normally they do not have any way of knowing the outcomes of the care plans, but in these cases they may be re-appointed some time later. This sometimes can be distressing, as the care plan may not have been carried out for various reasons.

The research (DHSS, 1985) indicates that care can be a damaging experience. There are two recent case examples of which I am aware where guardians were re-appointed to find that the care plans had not been carried out.

In one case, a 10-month-old boy was made subject to a care order with a plan for adoption. Five years later the guardian was re-appointed because the father had made an application for contact. The child was still placed with the same short-term foster carer he had been with at the time of the care proceedings. There was no obvious reason why he had not been found a permanent placement, but finding one for him at the age of 5, when he had become attached to his foster carer and was showing signs of disturbance at the prospect of being moved, was going to be much more difficult. This carer was not able to keep him herself. The guardian was very critical of the local authority, as was the court.

In another case, a care plan on a 4-year-old girl recommended an attempt at rehabilitation and this was agreed at the final hearing. Four years later the guardian was re-appointed in a contact application, to find that the girl had been in a short-term placement for two-and-a-half years following an unsuccessful rehabilitation attempt, with no permanent family on the horizon and the current placement was under considerable strain.

These two examples highlight the potential for drift in cases once care orders are made and the children are considered safe. The Department of Health has recently published reports on the inspection of selected local authorities' adoption and fostering services (SSI, 1996a; SSI 1996b), which does show that where adequate resources of senior management time were put into developing adoption services, this was of direct benefit to the children requiring these services. This same report also shows that prolonged court proceedings, leaving children's futures in doubt, prejudiced good quality planning. What may have been agreed as a care plan at the time of the final hearing has no guarantee of success and the above examples are not unusual in guardians' experience. They may be in part due to resource constraint, in a less obvious way than the previous examples.[1]

I would like to pose another question: is it the proper function of the guardian's role to undertake an enquiry into the local authority where they have failed to implement a care plan? Alternatively, should judges be more proactive in seeking explanations from the local authority by writing to the Director of Social Services to seek an explanation?

I have looked at case examples where it is the policies of the local authority which have led to conflict over care plans. There are also examples of which I am aware where guardians come across different views about social work practice. Sometimes there is an inability to make a decision, for example in a case involving two young siblings who had very different needs, the guardian assisted the social worker in making a decision to place them separately, which enabled a placement to be found for both and an agreed care plan at the final hearing.

CONFLICT OVER CONTACT

There are other examples where, while there may be agreement over the need for a care order, local authorities and guardians may be in conflict over contact issues. It is extremely difficult to fix a decision about contact at one point in time, when so many factors are likely to change. Local authorities are finding it increasingly difficult to recruit foster and adoptive parents. The view is taken by some family placement teams that adoptive parents will be resistant to direct contact with a child's natural parents. If a care plan is for adoption, the local authority often applies to terminate direct contact in order to make it easier to recruit a permanent substitute family.

The research findings (Adcock, 1995, p 20) show that the problem of maintaining links between absent child and parent is multi-dimensional. There is some evidence (Thoburn, 1996, p 132) that the total severance model whereby adopters had a fresh start with a child, was damaging to children since they had no sense of their origin. Local authorities now frequently operate post-box indirect contact for children but are resistant to direct contact particularly where a younger child is being placed. Policies which require all direct contact to cease before a permanent placement is sought for a child are often questioned by guardians. The individual child's needs must be considered first and it may be the guardian's task to ensure that the contact is appropriate to that child's needs rather than according to the local authority's policy for children in permanent placement.

THE ROLE OF THE GUARDIAN SERVICE IN COMMENTING ON LOCAL AUTHORITY PRACTICE

There is a potential role for guardians in commenting on local authority practice as it affects the children and families they come into contact with. The Department of Health encourages such a dialogue about policy and practice. The local authorities now have to produce Children's Services Plans and are encouraged to seek wider sources of information. Data collected by the GALRO service, which panel managers are required to compile into annual reports, would be a useful source.

In one local authority the guardians highlighted the effect the pursuance of a purchaser/provider split was having on children and families and were instrumental in changing this policy. This was done by systematically collecting information about the effect the policies were having on children and families with whom guardians were involved. This was presented in a report which was made available to councillors and was instrumental in effecting a change in policy.

GUARDIAN PRACTICE

I am conscious that I have concentrated on the practice of local authorities and not considered that of guardians. I am aware that some of the conflict between guardians and local authorities can be due to the

1 This issue of drift received considerable attention at the conference and the guardians present took the opportunity to meet together to consider appropriate ways forward. The results of that consideration are presented in a postscript.

practice of guardians themselves. Issues such as style, lack of boundaries, lack of realism, inadequately briefing themselves (Wheeler, 1995, p 42) have been identified as poor practice on the part of guardians. There is now a set of national standards (DoH, 1995) for the guardian service which are monitored by panel managers through annual reviews of guardians' work. Feedback about the guardian's performance is often sought from courts, social workers and sometimes families to assist in this process. These reviews are carried out without compromising the guardian's independence. All panels are required to have a complaints procedure in place and this can be used if there is concern about a guardian's practice. The regulations governing this procedure have recently been revised by the Panel Regulations Amendments 1997, following the recommendations of a Department of Health Working Party Report in 1996 (SSI, 1996c).

WAYS FORWARD

It is important that those who might find themselves in conflict are in a position to analyse where that conflict comes from – whether it is caused by financial constraints; the over-rigid application of a local authority policy; a difference between the opinion of an independent expert and that of the guardian; a difference of professional judgement between the social worker and the guardian; a problem of poor practice on the part of either the social worker and guardian; or even tensions arising out of the perceptions the social worker and guardian may have of each other. Identifying the source of the conflict may help to take out some of the heat and enable agreement to be achieved. If there is no agreement then at least the cooler identification of the issues will enable them to be put with greater clarity before the court and facilitate the court's task in deciding what is in the child's interest.

I have asked several guardians what they look for in an ideal care plan. The following are some suggestions:

- There should be clear communication with everyone, especially the family.
- There should be a long-term view which includes what work will be done with the child.
- While the structure of the format in the Guidance (DoH, 1991) should be followed, this should not be allowed to lead to a rigidity of content within each section which fails to allow for the individual characteristics of the child concerned.
- The care plan should reflect the individual child's needs, not corporate policy.
- There should be precision in some areas, for example what resources will be made available (having ensured there is the finance agreed for these).
- Clear time-scales should be established.
- There should be consideration of what will happen if, for example, the plan for rehabilitation fails.
- Contact being a dynamic issue, the plan should consider what is right for the child currently, while recognising that this may change.

These suggestions are very similar to those in the Department of Health guide for social workers reporting to court (Plotnikoff and Wilson, 1996, ch 14) which also suggests that it may be necessary to acknowledge that a particular level of service is not available for resource reasons. It further advises against describing a resource-led decision as being in the child's interest unless it is so (ibid, p 76).

There has been a suggestion (Wheeler, 1995, p 41) that one way forward for guardians and social workers to ensure good communication while maintaining guardians' independence is to have a meeting between the guardian, the social worker, and the team manager at the beginning of a case to establish:

- how the guardian has access to relevant case information;
- time-scales for the work;
- what will be the process for negotiations regarding care plans; and
- how disagreements are to be resolved.

I understand that a protocol covering most of these aspects is being piloted in Yorkshire.[1] It is designed to ensure that social worker and guardian understand each other's position from the time they first encounter one another. The aim is to avoid conflict if at all possible. Making the range of possible

1 Available from the North Yorkshire and York Panel of Guardians ad Litem, PO Box 130, Haxby, York YO3 3XH.

sources of conflict clear will produce a greater chance of avoiding it. What remains will arise from real professional differences of opinion which should be put before the court for its decision.

Out of conflict can come creative and imaginative solutions which do not compromise the child's welfare. Hostility, rudeness and any degree of arrogance are not helpful. Conflict should lead to careful analysis, an objective review of the arguments and the humility to modify positions.

POSTSCRIPT

There was much discussion at the conference about whether there should be monitoring of cases after a care order has been made. The guardians who attended considered this and put forward the following as a possible means of avoiding children being left in situations of drift.

> The guardian could receive copies of reviews on the children for one year following the making of a care order. This would also enable monitoring to ensure that reviews take place. Statutory reviews must be held at one month, three months and six months following the accommodation of a child by a local authority (Review of Children's Cases Regulations 1991).
>
> The suggestion is that should the guardian, as a result of receiving these reviews, believe that the local authority is not carrying out the agreed care plan, then the case could be referred back to the court which heard the care proceedings. The duties of the guardian would be minimal, and would not include the visiting of prospective placements. The decision to return to court would only be made if all other avenues of negotiation had failed. There could then be a directions hearing to determine the way forward.
>
> It is at this stage difficult to know how many cases this would involve, since currently guardians only know about the cases to which they are re-appointed. It is felt that where local authorities have robust reviewing procedures drift is less likely to occur.

A further point might also be considered. The time-scale operating in cases which go to court means that once a final hearing has been held the one- and three-month statutory reviews may well have taken place and further reviews are not required any more frequently than six-monthly. Is this sufficiently frequent for the above proposal to be effective?

REFERENCES

Adcock, M (1995) 'Contact: An Overview', in Argent, H (ed) *See You Soon: Contact with children looked after by local authorities* (BAAF).

Booth, Dame M (1996) *Avoiding Delay in Children Act Cases* (LCD).

DHSS (1985) *Social Work Decisions in Child Care, Recent Research Findings and their Implications* (HMSO).

DoH (1991) *Children Act 1989 Guidance and Regulations*, vol 3, Family Placements para 262 p 15 (HMSO).

DoH (1995) *A Guide for Guardians ad Litem in Public Law Proceedings under the Children Act 1989* (HMSO).

Guardians ad Litem and Reporting Officers (Panels) Regulations 1983 (SI 1983/1908).

Guardians ad Litem and Reporting Officers (Panels) Regulations 1991 (SI 1991/2051).

Guardians ad Litem and Reporting Officers (Panels) (Amendment) Regulations 1997 (SI 1997/1662).

Plotnikoff, J and Wilson, R (1996) *Reporting to Court under the Children Act* (HMSO).

Review of Children's Cases Regulations 1991 (SI 1991/895).

SSI (1996a) *Inspection of Local Authority Adoption Services* (HMSO).

SSI (1996b) *Inspection of Local Authority Fostering 1995–6 National Summary Report* (HMSO).

SSI (1996c) *Complaints Working Party Report* (DoH).

Thoburn, J (1996) 'Psychological parenting and child placement: "But we want to have our cake and eat it" ' in Howe, D (ed) *Attachment and Loss in Child and Family Social Work* (Avebury) at p 129.

Wheeler, J (1995) 'A Social Services viewpoint on working together or apart from Guardians', in 5 (1995) *Seen and Heard* at p 38.

APPENDIX 1

Extending the review process

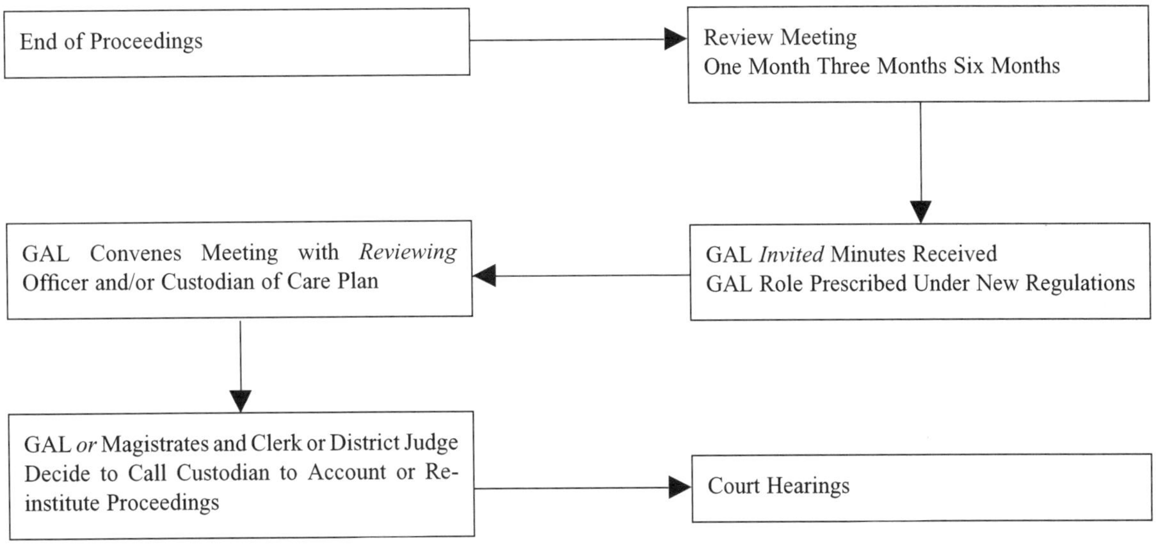

APPENDIX 2

GALRO Panel Activity Data 1 August 1995 to 31 July 1996

NOTE – ALL DEFINITIONS ARE THOSE USED IN THE DATA COLLECTION WORKING PARTY REPORT 1993

Type of appplication when GALRO appointed	Number of GALROs appointed	
1. Adoption (Guardian)	1115	8.48%
2. Adoption (Reporting Officer)	3274	24.90%
3. Freeing (Guardian)	398	3.03%
4. Freeing (Reporting Officer)	71	0.54%
5. Care	)5068	)38.54%
6. Supervision	)	)
7. Section 37 Direction	80	0.61%
8. Discharge Care Order or discharge SO	751	5.71%
9. Extension of Supervision Order	51	0.39%
10. Application s 39(4)	16	0.12%
11. Residence Order (for child subject to CO)	202	1.54%
12. Contact	594	4.52%
13. Emergency Protection	801	6.09%
14. Child Assessment	21	0.16%
15. Appeal	36	0.27%
16. Secure Accommodation	489	3.72%
17. Change of Surname	10	0.08%
18. Live Abroad	17	0.13%
19. Parental Order (s 30 HFE Act)	34	0.26%
20. Multiple Proceedings	56	0.43%
21. Other	66	0.50%
22. TOTAL	13150	

EIGHTH SESSION

'THE BEST LAID PLANS': LOCAL AUTHORITIES AND CARE PLANNING

Anne Chan and Gloria McFarlane
in consultation with Robert Hughes and Peter Murphy

SUMMARY OF PAPER

In introducing their paper, it was emphasised that there was a need to remember that all looked after children have to have care plans which are made and reviewed whether or not the case is going to court.

Audit

The conference was reminded that complaints systems exist, departments are subject to SSI inspections, there was the possibility of judicial review: there were all manner of audit mechanisms, both internal and external. Their own local authority was also consulting with looked after children by way of a questionnaire and there were a range of performance indicators to be reviewed which would provide triggers to further exploration where they were not being adequately met. In addition, there were the court-based avenues of review such as parents' contact applications, grandparents' applications for residence, local authority applications under section 34(4); all of which provide a means whereby the care plan is subject to reconsideration by the court.

Care Plans

It was important to remember that this was a snapshot at a particular point in time for a child and was subject to change as the child's needs changed and/or there was a change in circumstances.

Assessment

Anne Chan posed the question of when does one decide there has been enough assessment? This was an expensive and often slow process. There were the 'hopeless' cases where the proposal for further assessment has to be balanced against the problems created by further bonding between parents and child, raising parents' expectations and further delay.

Social Workers

It was important to remember that the social workers in care proceedings are generally qualified professionals and may have the advantage of having worked closely with the family for a considerable time in their own environment. No guardian could have the same intimate knowledge solely through their involvement in the court proceedings.

Conference participants should remember that there was no perfect care plan; no right or wrong plan and no perfect placement.

> 'The best laid schemes o' mice an' men
> Gang aft a-gley'
>
> 'To a mouse' (1786)
> Robert Burns 1759–96

With some 600 children looked after in the London Borough of Southwark we, as senior officers, have in this paper drawn upon our experience of the care planning process in all aspects, including its role in court proceedings. Southwark is an inner London multi-cultural local authority with 38% of its child population being from black and ethnic minority communities and ranks on socio-economic indicators as the second most deprived borough in the country.

Of the children looked after as at 31 March 1997, 223 were accommodated and 374 were on care orders, which places Southwark second highest nationally with 105 children looked after per 10,000 in the child population. These cases are managed by some 90 social workers and supported by eight social services lawyers, mostly dealing with child care matters.

In the period April to September 1997, section 31 applications were issued for 27 families involving 57 children. The number of cases current at the end of September was 42 families, involving 80 children which were allocated to the courts as follows: High Court 4; Principal Registry 17; Family Proceedings 21. There were also 56 interim care orders as at September 1997.

The local authority needs to have care plans for any child that it is looking after and these plans have to be reviewed at regular intervals. The Regulations apply whether there are court proceedings or not and therefore this review process operates in parallel with the court when there are proceedings. The Regulations, which are the Arrangements for Placement of Children Regulations, Placement of Children with Parents Regulations and Review of Children's Cases Regulations, refer, amongst other things, to the requirement to making arrangements for the welfare of a child, statutory reviews in specific time periods and considering the need for the care order (if any) to continue.

The courts need confidence in social services and we want to make some important assurances. First, the local authority's concern is the welfare of the child. Secondly, the local authority values the court process in helping to decide the best future for the child. Thirdly, at each stage the local authority will act with integrity, ie it will be open about its intentions and will fulfil as far as is possible its plans presented to the court. The care process requires confidence on the part of the court that this will be done – otherwise the courts will be tempted to prolong the interim stage, which may be to the detriment of the welfare of the child and contrary to the general principle on delay in section 1(2) of the Act.

In our view, once the court is satisfied that the section 31 threshold criteria have been met, the only decision of the court, under section 1(5), is whether the order recommended in the current care plan is better than any other order or no order at all for the child; it is not whether the care plan can be improved. Further interim orders to enable assessment or additional evidence should only be considered if the outcome is likely to assist the final order decision. There is a distinction to be made between evidence bearing on the court's role during the interim stage to enable a decision to be made and matters which bear on the future of the child once the final order is made but which do not affect that decision.

Local authorities, as of course do the courts, have difficult dilemmas such as how much assessment there needs to be before formulating a care plan to present to the court to enable a final decision to be made, how to judge the resource needs of one child against others known to have needs (and indeed against all the other obligations of the authority going beyond social services). Sometimes the local authority has been compelled to undertake further assessments utilising scarce resources on cases it believed to be 'hopeless' based on the history. Research as to whether the local authority is right in these cases would be helpful.

The case of A, B and C

A baby had a spiral fracture; mother and father said the four-year-old boy was responsible. Mother and father and baby (under an interim care order) and the two boys aged two and four (no order but proceedings) were placed in a local authority residential assessment unit; the parents were also undergoing parental assessment by a family centre. There were such concerns raised about the father that he was referred to the Maudsley for a risk assessment. The Maudsley said that the father was such a risk to the children that he could never be considered as a long-term carer and there was no point in continuing the assessment. The mother refused to leave the father, emergency protection orders followed by interim care orders were obtained on the boys and the children were placed with foster carers. There was a four-month gap until the final hearing; the local authority prepared a care plan based on the assessments – basically adoption though unsure as to whether the whole sibling group should be placed together which would depend on the timescale to find such a placement. On the Friday before the hearing on the Monday, the local authority received the guardian ad litem's report recommending a further assessment of mother and father as carers for the four-year-old (the alleged perpetrator) and criticised the local authority for not doing any further assessment in the four-month period – she had not raised any of this previously with the local authority. A ten-day final hearing led to three care orders being made. This case emphasises that the assessment of the family is connected with the decision to make a care order or not, not for argument about the local authority's management of the case.

In most cases where an application is issued, the family will be well known to the local authority, perhaps for a long time. The social worker is also likely to have a specific and intimate knowledge of the family and their environment which aids good assessment and care planning. If a care order is made, the local authority will have statutory duties for implementing it and exercising the parental responsibility which this carries. We think this means that the courts should consider carefully before substituting a plan, eg from the guardian ad litem or expert witness, based (as it usually is) on a time-limited and more superficial knowledge of the family and sometimes a particular perspective on how children are best cared for. This is not to say of course that the local authority's intentions should not be properly tested by the court. The local authority will accept an improvement to its plan with gratitude (and the possibility of improving the plan can perhaps be seen as an important but secondary effect of the court process), but if it agrees to changes in the plan only under pressure from the court against its better judgement, while it will no doubt do its best, the result is not likely to be the optimum.

The perception is – there is no data that we are aware of – that the section 31 criteria is conceded in the majority of cases, and in some even the care order is conceded. Most argument in court is centred on the care plan and contact. In many cases, the care plan is not an issue between the local authority, court and guardian ad litem and, in some cases, not even the parents disagree. However, in a considerable number of cases brought by our authority, around one-half, there is disagreement about the care plan which prolongs the court process, even though there is no disagreement that a care order should be made. This has tended to be associated with proposals by the guardian ad litem or expert witness for independent fostering arrangements instead of a local authority foster family or for a residential assessment of the family before the care order is made. Valuable though these may be for some children, they require special justification in the light of the resources absorbed if they are to be used more commonly.

A particular independent fostering scheme or a particular family fostering under such a scheme may have a special value for a particular child, but this should be the local authority's decision in the light of all the circumstances, and delay in reaching agreement on this does not justify court adjournment if the court is already satisfied that the care order is required. We hope the conference will agree that argument about the care plan should be clearly relevant to the court's decision on whether to make the order sought.

We would like now to describe some case examples relevant to the themes we are addressing.

The case of D

D, aged four, was the subject of a three-day hearing in January of this year. The court heard a background of mother's alcohol misuse and mental health problems. The application was opposed by the mother. The local authority, with the agreement of the guardian ad litem and two expert witnesses, argued that delay to test further the mother's ability to care for D would not be appropriate – the interests of the child would be found in achieving a permanent substitute family.

The magistrate agreed and a care order made. In April, the case was presented to the adoption panel and a decision made that adoption was in the child's best interests. Three potential adoptive placements had been identified. A matter of only two weeks later D's maternal grandfather made an application for leave to apply for a residence order as a sole carer for D following a significant change in his personal circumstances. Although he was known to social services he was unable to care for D at the time of the proceedings because he was caring for an elderly relative; that relative had recently died, hence his availability to care for D. In the first week of June, D's mother filed an application for discharge of the care order.

In this case the care plan was clear and unequivocal in its focus upon the needs of the child as then seen, but this changed rapidly with the new circumstances. For D these changes proved positive and she is now living with her grandfather under the care order. He has withdrawn his application for leave; the mother has withdrawn her application to discharge the care order and has contact for three hours unsupervised every Sunday afternoon.

Although it is early days, these changes have so far proved positive. However, in other circumstances, such changes can have serious consequences with children experiencing extended periods in short-term foster placements where, inevitably, their attachment will deepen. For the local authority the resource issues are significant. Valuable resources, including a blocked short-term foster placement, may be diverted from the pursuit of the child's best interests to contend with post-order applications.

The case of E and F

E, boy, and F, girl, aged nine and ten, were accommodated in May 1995 against a background of mother's serious alcohol misuse and neglect of the children. Care proceedings were initiated in September 1995 when mother's detox attempt failed with care orders granted in June 1996. The care plan envisaged the placement of the children together within a long-term substitute family. Contact was at the discretion of the local authority. By the time of the making of the order, the children had already experienced four placements as a result of their and the mother's disruptive behaviour. One placement had to be terminated because of criminal damage caused by the mother to the foster carer's house; in addition, the mother telephoned the foster carers at all hours, usually intoxicated and abusive. Shortly after the making of the order, F expressed a wish to be placed separately from E – a view accepted by the local authority in the context of F's dramatically escalating behavioural problems, including violent and sexualised behaviour, and the negative impact it was having on E. E is currently in a local authority children's home and a long-term foster placement is being sought.

F was placed in a specialist foster home but this placement was disrupted in October 1996; subsequently she was placed in a specialist small residential unit with additional resources provided by the local authority to ensure F received a greater level of adult supervision and attention. This placement then broke down and F was placed in the local authority's own residential unit for this age group but when that broke down, she was placed in a highly regarded therapeutic unit: that placement is also now breaking down. The search for a suitable placement, which will be her ninth, continues with involvement from the guardian ad litem (in the contact application) and professional agencies. In response to firm controls on her level of contact, the mother made an application for increased contact; a cross-application by the local authority for leave to refuse contact was made and was granted.

The details of this case emphasise the changing needs of the child and how a local authority must necessarily respond, despite the initial intentions of the care plan. Intensive support work has been undertaken with F and her many carers, but there are no ready-made solutions to the extremes of need F exhibits. On occasion ourselves and, we believe, other local authorities receive criticism from guardians ad litem for an apparent reluctance to commit resources – typically around commissioning expensive placements in the independent sector. This case also exemplifies the willingness of the local authority to commit substantial resources in the search for stability and, ultimately, permanency for F. But non-local authority resources are, we believe, too often seen as a panacea for the complex and deep-seated needs of the child. Currently, F's future remains uncertain.

The cases of D, E and F were in the family proceedings court because the issues relating to the section 31 criteria were relatively simple; the subsequent issues relating to the care plans are not.

The case of G

G, aged nine, is one of a sibling group of four accommodated in October 1995 from the sole care of father who had been unable to cope despite intensive support. The mother has considerable drug misuse problems. Care proceedings commenced in July 1996 as it became apparent that rehabilitation would not be possible. Initially, it was hoped to place the children in pairs but this proved incompatible with their individual care needs. While the other children settled reasonably well into their care settings (a mixture of local authority and agency foster carers) G's behaviour was cause for concern and resulted in four placement breakdowns before a more stable short-term placement was achieved with a short-term local authority foster carer.

At the final hearing in November 1996, the local authority's care plan acknowledged that meeting G's care needs would involve a complex set of arrangements. The care plan reflected this by proposing a 'mixed economy' of provision based upon external resources, ie specialist school and therapy, supporting a local authority long-term foster placement which was yet to be identified. The guardian ad litem disagreed, arguing that G would benefit from an integrated support package of a type available from some private fostering organisations; such a package had been of benefit to one of the siblings.

However, throughout the proceedings the guardian ad litem failed to identify or distinguish between G's short- and long-term needs and how these were to be matched to an appropriate placement. At the final hearing, the district judge determined that orders would be made in respect of the other three children with an interim order in respect of G.

Following the directions of the district judge, the local authority contacted five organisations deemed to have the potential to meet G's care needs. Two of the five felt unable to meet G's needs, while the other three had no vacancies. Simultaneously, in January of this year, a local authority long-term placement was identified and work commenced on matching G's additional support needs with local resources, much of which was already in place as the long-term placement was in close proximity to her current short-term placement and would not even require a change of school. The guardian ad litem continued to oppose the local authority's plan without having any clear alternative to offer. A care order was made in late March of this year based upon the original proposals placed before the court by the local authority, albeit with an identified foster carer.

In this case, G revealed from an early stage that her needs would exceed the capacity of any placement that did not have an extensive package of support attached to it. Such a package need not necessarily be with agency foster carers, there are alternatives as shown here. The local authority was equally mindful of the need to promote within G a sense of permanency with plans that identified a clear and purposeful route towards achieving this. Sometimes this will take time – we are acutely aware of the need to hold timescales to a minimum, but we also recognise that if complex needs are to be effectively met, then time is well spent on achieving a placement that offers the chance of sustaining itself over the longer term.

These three cases give illustrations of care planning and the need to adapt as necessary.

In the first, an unexpected change in circumstances caused us to try a different option of care for the child. This can be achieved anyway under the care order but, in this case, would have come up for 'review' by the court in considering the grandfather's and the mother's applications.

In the second, changes in the behaviour of the children under a care order caused the local authority to seek different and more elaborate types of placement. This will not, in itself, come back to court but will have some relevance in the context of the hearing on contact.

The third, exemplifies the type of argument which can take place between the guardian ad litem and the local authority even though the need for a care order is not disputed.

These cases also provide examples of potential avenues for a review of the local authority's care plan – applications by parents for contact or discharge, applications by grandparents for residence orders, applications by a local authority for leave to refuse contact to a child in care pursuant to section 34(4). In all these types of cases – and they are increasing – the court can see what the local authority has done to implement the care plan and the application may lead to a change in the plan.

Research under way by Professor Judith Harwin of the University of Sussex is looking at the fate of care plans as presented to the court, and until that is completed, it is impossible to estimate how many care plans are amended post order and why.

During the time between issuing the section 31 application and the final hearing, whether there are interim care orders or the child is accommodated or the child remains at home, it is essential there should be an interim care plan. For example, an interim care plan that recommends rehabilitation should have a strict programme that all parties are aware of; the plan should be monitored and reviewed, possibly at an interim or directions hearing, so that by the time of the final hearing, hopefully it will be known if the plan has been successful or not and it should be possible for the local authority to present a realistic care plan to the court at the final hearing.

We would suggest that the Children Act envisaged a court process involving a relatively speedy final hearing. One year into the Children Act, Southwark had a case where a nine-year-old killed a two-year-old when he was left alone with her and three other children younger than him. There was never any doubt that a care order would be made, but at a directions appointment when the local authority applied to adjourn the final hearing for assessment of the child to assist in determining the type of placement, the delay was not acceptable to the court who suggested the local authority should seek the order and incorporate the assessment into its care plan. A very different scenario it would seem from the one we now have.

If there is delay in the making of the final order, there are likely to be repercussions for the child and the care planning process in that the child may begin to form an attachment to the short-term carer, may develop behavioural problems due to the uncertainty and become more difficult to place in the long term. We refer you to the case of G in our paper in which we believe delay in making the final order was detrimental to the child and that delay did not assist any of the parties.

The court process itself can be very demanding on the local authority in terms of resources of managers, lawyers, social workers etc, so that we must be sure that only those orders which are necessary are applied for and that so far as the local authority is concerned the procedures are properly followed with all due speed. Examples of total legal costs to the local authority are as follows:

Family proceedings court (2-day final hearing)	£4,000
Principal Registry (1-day final hearing)	£6,000
High Court (8-day final hearing)	£23,000

All legal costs in care proceedings in Southwark come out of the social services budget; if resources are directed to legal costs, there is less available for other front line services.

It should also be borne in mind that specialist assessments in independent placements are costly; examples are:

Residential assessment for parents and two children	£2,700 per week
Specialist foster placement for one child	£1,055 per week

Short-term placements are more expensive than long-term ones: where there is uncertainty as to when the final order will be made, places sometimes have to be kept open with the attendant costs and possible placements blockages.

We sense some anxiety on the part of the court that because post-order activity is beyond the intervention of the court (unless there are subsequent proceedings) it may wish to ensure that the care plan presented to the court at the final hearing is as 'cast iron' as possible. For this reason, the local authority should be as realistic and honest as it can be and if, for example, it is likely to take, say, two years to place a child with special needs for adoption, then the care plan must say so.

It should be remembered that care plans are approximations of the child's best interests. There is no perfect plan when dealing with the complex and dynamic needs and circumstances of a child. A care plan for any child will derive from a range of factors and information sources which includes opinions from expert witnesses and the guardian ad litem but, most importantly, will represent the assessment skills of the social workers who will take all the available information into account. Furthermore, the care plan, amended if need be during the interim process, represents the best view of the local authority at one point in time.

As already stated, local authorities have statutory duties and parental responsibility for children in their care which includes the requirement to review cases at specified intervals. However, more can and must be done to ensure that care planning remains child-centred, focused upon clear objectives and timescales and contain a realistic appraisal of the needs of the child as well as the resources required to meet them. Such an approach is vital to the post-order stage but is not unique to it. Indeed, the characteristics of effective care planning must be embedded from the very beginning; they must continue throughout the uncertainties of the legal process and act as a solid platform for realising the objectives of the care plan at the post-order stage. It should be remembered that if there is non-co-operation from the parents, no long-term placement, whether it be long-term foster care or adoption, can be effected until there is a care order.

An example of the review process post-order is a case where three children aged five, seven and 12, were subject to care orders, and the care plan recommended a permanent substitute family. The mother had a chronic drink problem but, following the proceedings, she responded to treatment, formed a stable relationship and the children were placed back with her. The local authority is now applying to discharge the care orders. It is not perfect, but the children are receiving good care and are where they want to be.

Additionally, our approach supports the idea of continuous planning that is not confined to the statutory review; social workers and their managers are expected to 'fine tune' care plans between reviews so as to guard against 'drift'.

The care planning process for all children looked after by the local authority is receiving a lot of attention. Some three-quarters of all authorities, including ours, are now using the Department of Health's 'Looking After Children' Assessment and Action Records. These care planning materials provide a systematic way of keeping track of a child's progress on seven dimensions of development, including health, education, social skills and behaviour. Apart from providing some degree of standardisation nationally, these will help local authorities to make the care planning process for individual children more effective by taking into account a broad review of a child's progress. The 'Looking After Children' materials will also provide a rich source of data for future service planning. Alongside this initiative, we recognise the importance of social workers being familiar with research evidence and its implications for good practice and have invested substantially in training programmes in this area.

Placement stability is crucial if the ambitions of the care plan are to be realised. Research evidence on the breakdown of substitute family care is well known. We now place greater emphasis on post-placement support, our primary objective being to support placements against breakdown. Support includes dedicated psychological and psychiatric resources that address the specific needs of the child and also provide ongoing advice to the carer. Meeting children's needs cannot be the remit solely of social services; making a care plan work requires the commitment of other services, particularly health, education and housing. There is ample evidence that where services collaborate the prognosis of looked after children is improved.

There have been proposals that the court should review care plans and some criteria have been suggested. In our opinion, this will cause further delay and poses a number of questions – when will a final order be final, how can the local authority plan for the period prior to the review, how will the criteria be established, how will the process be resourced, what powers will the court be given over local authority duties? A care order is a care order whether it is made in the family proceedings court, Principal Registry or High Court; any review will lead to significant cost implications. The courts, especially the higher courts, now have difficulty listing final hearings in good time: if they also have to hear reviews of care plans, what are the implications for court lists?

If a local authority fails to comply with its statutory obligations in respect of children looked after, there are already procedures which can be invoked; for example, complaints procedures and applications for judicial review by parents, children, and carers. In addition, all social services departments are subject to scrutiny by the Department of Health's Social Services Inspectorate and the Audit Commission. Then there is also ultimately the power of referral to the Secretary of State to consider implementing his default powers. Concerns that a local authority is not implementing a care plan, for whatever reason, should be a matter, in our view, considered outside of the care proceedings arena unless there are subsequent Children Act applications such as contact or discharge.

Drawing these themes together, we would wish to emphasise the long-term accountability of the local authority for the outcome of care plans in respect of individual children. In exercising this responsibility, the local authority would be assisted by a recognition that it will encounter difficulties, and sometimes situations, that may require significant adjustments to the care plan presented to the court, if post-order care planning is to be in the best interests of the child in the longer-term.

For the local authority, the care plan at the final hearing stage is a milestone – albeit a very important one – on what for many children will be a much longer journey. It is important to remember that there are many care plans which are followed through as presented to the court, as exemplified by one of our recent cases where the seventh and eighth children of a sibling group were placed for adoption together within three months of a care order. Fundamentally, our task is to ensure that the child is supported by a planning process that can respond quickly to changing needs and circumstances as well as provide stability to safeguard and promote the child's welfare.

At the same time, as the standard of local authority care improves, so we hope the courts will have more confidence in the local authority's ability to carry out its plans, amending them as necessary in the interests of the child.

> 'Nothing in progress can rest on its original plan. We may as well think of rocking a grown man in the cradle of an infant.'
>
> Letter to the Sheriffs of Bristol 1777
> Edmund Burke 1729–97

NINTH SESSION

CARE PLANNING: AN INTER-AGENCY ENDEAVOUR: OBSERVATIONS

Professor Judith Harwin

INTRODUCTION

The importance of care planning: the approach of the Children Act 1989

In 1971, in an address[1] to the National Children's Home Convocation, Professor Roy Parker argued that children in public care, perhaps more than any other group, required stability and continuity in their lives. This in turn laid on social workers an expectation to plan for what Parker called 'preferred futures'. By this he meant the careful consideration of desirable and feasible options for each child in care, with a commitment to both short and longer-term planning. In contrast to this statement of the ideal, he noted, was the far commoner reality of a failure to make long-term plans or indeed, to plan at all. A steady stream of research published throughout the 1980s documented the continuing vulnerability of children in the care system and drew attention to drift, delay and the poor welfare outcomes of children in the care system.[2]

Although some steps were introduced to strengthen the planning process in the 1980s, the Children Act 1989 was the first piece of legislation to strengthen the care planning process systematically and comprehensively. First, it strengthened existing mechanisms of local authority review for all looked after children (whether or not on a court order) and introduced complaints procedures to heighten local authority accountability. The Department of Health also published detailed guidance on review procedures which covered, inter alia, requirements for their purpose, their timing, and participatory rights of children and parents.

At the same time the plans of the local authority for children it is seeking to look after via a court order acquired greater significance than before 1989. The Children Act introduced a new duty for the court to consider whether the making of an order will promote the child's welfare better than no order. To help reach its decision, the court needs to be informed of the intentions of the local authority and the care plan is the mechanism for doing this. Its role at this stage is most important because it influences the likelihood of the order being made or not. The care plan provides a framework for local authority case management and it delineates the goals to be achieved and the desired outcomes for the child.

The care plan is not at present enshrined in primary legislation and its influence is subtle and complex. The care plan is expected to be presented in good faith and to represent a reasonable account of the local authority's intentions. But there is no binding obligation on the local authority to adhere to the care plan as originally drawn up at the time of the application. Although guidance by the Department of Health determines the areas to be covered, there are no detailed criteria laid down to establish what constitutes an adequate plan. To date it has been left to some important court judgments[3] and good practice, assisted by a new DH handbook *Reporting to Court under the Children Act*[4] to help clarify expectations as to the status and quality of care plans.

The status and quality of care plans have, however, been only one aspect of the debates that have taken place since the Children Act 1989 on care planning. A related, but far broader question, has been whether the legislation drew the boundaries correctly between the powers of the social services and the courts. Under the 1989 Act the courts have no role in relation to the care of a child unless the question arises of the discharge of the care order or unless some other order such as discharge is an issue. The

1 Parker, R A (1971) *Planning for Deprived Children*, National Children's Home, Harpenden.
2 DHSS (1985) *Social Work Decisions in Child Care: Recent Research Findings and their Implications*, HMSO.
3 *Manchester City Council v F* [1993] 1 FLR 419; *Re J (Minors) (Care: Care Plan)* [1994] 1 FLR 253.
4 Plotnikoff, J and Woolfson, R (1996) *Reporting to Court under the Children Act*, DH, HMSO, London.

question whether the courts should review the care of a child subject to a care order has been examined in a number of fora.[1] Yet only in 1994/95 the Children Act Advisory Committee *Annual Report*[2] concluded that:

> 'it is clear that substantive evidence is required that difficulties are actually occurring before it would be appropriate for the SSI to consider undertaking a study of the issue or for any change in the court's powers to be considered.'

At that point it did not seem as though enough evidence was available. Yet one of the proposals put forward at the start of this conference by some judges was for some form of post-care order review. What has brought about this change in mood? The purpose of this paper is threefold: first, by drawing on existing research evidence, it considers whether there is 'substantive evidence' of difficulties. Secondly, it will consider how far a change in the law or institutional functions would be able to resolve the problems surrounding care planning. In the final section, other options will be discussed which may help achieve the fundamental objective – the promotion of the welfare of one of the most vulnerable groups in society.

IS THERE SUBSTANTIVE EVIDENCE THAT DIFFICULTIES ARE OCCURRING?

Since the Children Act Advisory Group reported in 1994/95 the situation has moved on. In the last few years the SSI[3] has been commissioned to carry out an inquiry into care planning for the courts and two other studies have also be funded by the Department of Health on the same theme. Unfortunately, none of these have been published yet, but Arran Poyser's study for the SSI and Joan Hunt and Alison Macleod's research for the Department of Health[4] will be available in the near future. The third study, which is being carried out at Sussex University and also has the support of the Lord Chancellor's Department,[5] is due to report at the end of 1999. Taken together, these three inquiries will all provide valuable evidence of the operation of the care planning system. They are already able to shed some light on a number of the concerns that case-law, the Children Act Advisory Group and Dame Margaret Booth's report[6] have highlighted. Also relevant is Roger Grimshaw and Dr Ruth Sinclair's inquiry *Planning and Reviewing Under the Children Act 1989*[7] because it analyses the way in which local authorities are discharging their obligations to review and plan for looked after children.

The research has set out to investigate a number of key themes. All of the studies mentioned above have commented on the status and quality of care plans, although Grimshaw and Sinclair's research does not focus exclusively on plans submitted to courts. This study, and also Hunt and Macleod's, include plans for children subject to alternative orders or no orders at all. Another link between the studies is that they have all incorporated into their design an examination of post-order case management by social services, using a mixture of file studies and questionnaires or interviews with social work personnel.

The views of judges and magistrates have helped to inform both the Sussex and SSI studies. The Sussex inquiry also entails detailed interviews with social workers, guardians and local authority solicitors and parents and older children will be interviewed at a later stage. The Sussex study is prospective, and it will attempt to examine welfare outcomes as well as outcome in terms of plan implementation at the end of an 18-month period.

Quality and status of care plans

The findings from the existing studies are remarkably consistent. There seems to be broad agreement that care plans are now better formulated and fuller than in the early 1990s. The researchers have noted with approval that, today, care plans are usually separate documents, frequently with one plan for each

---

1 See, for example, articles by Hayes, M (1996) 'The proper role of courts in child care cases', *Child and Family Law Quarterly*, vol 8, no 3, pp 201–216; Brasse, G (1995) 'After the care order – into forbidden territory' Parts I and II *Family Law* January and February issues; Smith, C (1997) 'Judicial power and local authority discretion – the contested frontier' *Child and Family Law Quarterly*, vol 9, no 3, pp 243–257.

2 The Children Act Advisory Committee *Annual Report 1994/1995* p 37.

3 Department of Health Social Services Inspectorate 'Monitoring the Children Act 1989' *Court Order Study – Care Planning*.

4 Hunt, J and Macleod, A (forthcoming) *The Best Laid Plans: Outcomes of Judicial Decisions in Child Protection Cases*, HMSO.

5 Harwin, J and Owen, M *A Study to Investigate Implementation of Care Orders Made under the Children Act 1989*. This study is funded by the Department of Health.

6 Dame Margaret Booth (1996) *Avoiding Delay in Children Act Cases*, Lord Chancellor's Department, London.

7 Grimshaw, R and Sinclair, R (1997) *Planning to Care*, National Children's Bureau, London.

child of the family, whereas previously it was common to find the care plan incorporated into the main statement. In the preliminary findings of the Sussex study, the existing guidance from the Department of Health was considered by interviewees to provide an entirely satisfactory framework. Nevertheless, a number of concerns also emerged in the research. Solicitors and guardians ad litem in the study by Hunt and Macleod commented on the variability of standards in care planning. In the SSI study, the judiciary commented that care plans are sometimes too long, but in other cases too short. In the Sussex study, the key concerns to emerge at an early stage were that care plans lacked sufficient detail and specificity and were sometimes over-optimistic in their goals, especially with regard to adoptive placements, which resulted in unrealistic time-scales.

The Sussex study has been able to test out the opinion evidence obtained from the judiciary by analysing the content and form of 50 care plans put to the courts in 1997. While these have the advantage of representing the latest practice in a rapidly evolving field, it should be emphasised that this study is still in progress and the findings are therefore of a preliminary nature.

The framework outlined in Volume 3 of the *Children Act 1989 Guidelines and Regulations*[1] seems to have been universally adopted as a vehicle for presenting care plans to the court in the same local authorities. Although there are attendant dangers in the adoption of a 'laundry list' approach, this streamlining of decision-making has clearly been helpful in bringing about greater consistency in care plan formulation. Children's identified needs, which head the agenda, were carefully documented in most of the care plans studied, and there was often a clear line of continuity back to the welfare checklist which appeared in earlier social work statements.

However, there were also some indications that the care plans fell short of judicial expectations in certain important respects. Of the 20 areas listed in the DH guidance, four or five were regularly omitted. In particular, there was a tendency to omit time-scales and details of the placement, which were frequently mentioned by the judiciary as important ingredients of a good care plan, and to omit or give little information on long-term contact plans and the conditions which would be necessary for reunification. Time-scales were most likely to be provided for adoption, but not for other forms of long-term placement, while duration was usually one specified in respect of people approaching independence. Finally, and importantly, contingency plans, which were provided in more than one-half of the care plans studied, often lacked detail. In most cases the plan simply stated that recourse would be made to an administrative meeting if the placement were to break down, or else that another placement of a similar type would be sought.

There were some other indications that the full potential of the care plan is not being fully realised, although the judiciary did not raise these matters. For example, the Sussex analysis found that more information could have been provided on children's racial and cultural needs. These were mentioned in only about one-half of the cases where children were black or of mixed parentage, and in these cases more detail could have been anticipated. There was also a tendency to treat a number of other categories set out in the DH guidance in a routine manner. Frequently, the requirement to state the kind of support to be provided in the placement simply named the worker. The same approach was adopted when discussing the allocation of responsibility for implementation of the plan: often only the social worker, manager or the agency were mentioned. The only exception to this pattern was if the child was to be placed back home with birth parents, when a far fuller description of the expectations on the parent was set out, similar to the approach found in written agreements. Two other matters which tended to be filled in routinely were the arrangements for input into decision-making and for notifying the responsible authority of disagreements or making representations.

These findings need to be considered together with the available evidence on the concern that the local authority may vary a care plan after the making of an order either through bad faith or lack of resources or, alternatively, fail to expedite the plan with due speed. The best evidence to date on implementation of plans to courts comes from the study by Hunt and Macleod *The Best Laid Plans: Outcomes of Judicial Decisions in Child Protection Cases*. This research, which followed up 131 of the 133 children previously studied in the author's Statutory Intervention Project, found 'scant evidence of local authorities treating the overall objectives of care plans in cavalier fashion'. With specific regard to the 74 sample children on care orders, only six suffered a change of plan prior to placement. Furthermore,

1 Department of Health (1991) *The Children Act 1989 Guidance and Regulations* Volume 3 'Family Placements', para 2.62.

the study found that more than four out of five care plans for children on care orders were both implemented and achieved. However, as the authors acknowledge, this study was conducted at a time when care plans still lacked the kind of detail that is now expected by the courts. This may have meant that it was easier to achieve the plan because it tended to be couched in very general terms. The findings of the Sussex study should help to determine whether a very detailed plan which has been offered to the court tends to present problems at the stage of implementation or whether it provides exactly the kind of framework which is helpful in later management of the case.

More worryingly, however, Hunt found evidence of slippage in care plan implementation and a failure of plans at a later stage because of placement breakdown. Although not a primary focus of the research, the study also found disturbing evidence of failure to allocate social workers, frequent turnover of social workers and delay in reviews. Moreover, the care plans did not work out for two in five children on care orders, although it is important to note that new plans were made and implemented for the majority, a small number of children having moved on to a third or fourth plan. A significant minority, numbering eight of the 25 children who were not placed initially or who experienced placement breakdown, still remained unplaced at the end of the study.

These findings need to be seen in relation to their sister studies. Harwin and Owen's research too has found some preliminary evidence of slippage in the early implementation phase, although it is too early to judge its extent or long-term impact. Sinclair and Grimshaw also found evidence of problems in implementing plans within the time-scales set by a review – not least because time-scales often were not set and, among social workers, they found a widespread disbelief in the feasibility of attaching time-scales to placement plans. When the various elements of the review plans were disaggregated in the study by Sinclair and Grimshaw, implementation was found to be patchy. The highest rates of implementation were for legal and placement decisions (over 80%) but moderate rates were found for education (67%) followed by health and miscellaneous services (61% and 60% respectively) and the lowest rate was for contact decisions (45%). No significant differences were found in the implementation of plans for children on care orders when compared with those who were accommodated.

Discussion

What conclusions should be drawn from these findings and do they constitute evidence of 'substantive difficulties'? The most obvious point to emerge is that the picture is very mixed. Both judicial opinion evidence and the research into practice show causes for both optimism and concern. On the positive side, it is quite clear that the care planning framework is valued and the standard of plans presented to the courts seems to be improving. Indeed Poyser concludes from his inquiry that 'in general the care planning process is working'. Hunt's study should provide some reassurance to the courts that the plan presented is the one that is most likely to be implemented. The more disturbing evidence is of slippage, unexpected variation and, finally, for children on care orders, relatively high breakdown rates. All these latter findings must surely be seen as 'substantive' in terms of the likely impact on the child's future welfare.

The significance of the content analysis of social service care plans is harder to evaluate at this point. In the first place, as noted above, it will be important to establish the reasons for the lack of specificity in the areas discussed earlier before judging their significance. But there is a far more important point: the real test is whether a direct correlation can be found between a good quality care plan, active case management and a positive welfare outcome for the child. Conversely, it needs to be established whether a plan lacking in specificity is more likely to lead to *laissez faire* case management leading to poor welfare outcomes. These complex relationships are under exploration in the Sussex study but the findings will only be available in 1999. At present the common sense and very plausible assumption is that there is a correlation between these variables, but for the present the proposition remains untested. Moreover, a wide range of other variables are all likely to exert their influence on the child's welfare outcome and understanding this complex interplay will provide a far firmer basis for developing criteria by which to judge the quality of care plans than exists at present. One of the major aims of the Sussex study is to analyse these wide-ranging determinants of outcome. In this respect the findings of a

1994 SSI study *Planning Long Term Placements*[1] are noteworthy. For as well as the more widely recognised problems of scarce resources, a number of other key factors hindered implementation of long-term plans. These issues included changes of mind by parents, family opposition to the plan, court delays and contact-related issues. How far these factors (with the exception of court delays) could have been anticipated when the care plan was drawn up is obviously highly pertinent.

In short, the available research evidence corroborates certain practitioner concerns, most notably in relation to post-care order implementation. These issues undoubtedly constitute substantive difficulties but how far these problems are directly attributable to the quality of the care plan or to defects within the planning system as a system is not yet clear. Nor do we know what are the effects of delay or unplanned changes on the welfare outcome of the child. This will be examined in the Sussex study. In the meantime, given evidence of practitioner concerns, combined with the indications that there are some real difficulties in achieving the goals of planning after the making of the order, the proposal of the conference to alter court powers to include a monitoring role post care order will now be examined.

HOW FAR WOULD A CHANGE IN THE ROLE AND FUNCTIONS OF THE COURTS BE ABLE TO ADDRESS THE DIFFICULTIES?

The conference has put forward of wealth of ideas to improve the care planning system. Undoubtedly, the proposal put forward by some of the judges to introduce some form of post-care order court review would have the most far-reaching implications by shifting the boundaries between courts and social services. This possible procedure is outlined in detail in Arran Poyser's paper and therefore will be restated here only very briefly to enable a critique of the proposal from the perspective of both principle and feasibility.

The main proposition is to put in place a new power for a post-care order review which could be set in motion at any point in the year following the making of the order. It is envisaged that the review power will be used only in exceptional circumstances when, following scrutiny of all case conference minutes and local authority review meetings, the guardian reaches the view that (and I quote from Poyser's paper):

- the change in the detail of the plan is significantly contrary to the welfare of the child;
- unforeseen circumstances make the care plan inappropriate;
- the local authority is unable to implement the care plan as originally presented when the care order was made.

The guardian ad litem or the local authority would initiate the review and the power would be confined to the ratification of a new care plan which would be prepared by the local authority. This plan would be presented to the court with a separate report by the guardian. All those with parental responsibility would be notified and entitled to take part, with legal aid support (*source*: Arran Poyser, chapter 7).

There are two ways of looking at these proposals. The first view is that the proposed measures are a light-handed approach to address concerns over delay and drift in implementation. They would also provide a mechanism for review of plans made when the court has some concern over the plan, but no realistic alternative if the child's safety is to be ensured. Of the small number of cases that are expected to meet the criteria, an even smaller number would be likely to return to court because the guardian would be required to discuss the case with social services first to see what changes could be made without recourse to the courts.

According to the second view, the proposals are more radical than may be indicated by the numbers likely to be involved, because they would entail a shift from several principles underpinning the Children Act. First, these measures would alter the present status of the care plan, which according to present law is under the control of the local authority at the implementation stage. They would only make sense if the present status of the plan were altered to make it mandatory. More broadly, the proposed measures would also redraw occupational boundaries by giving courts and their officers (the guardians) an ongoing role in supervision and monitoring, instead of confining their interventions to adjudication. Such a shift would affect the notion of parental responsibility presently accorded to local

1 Department of Health Social Services Inspectorate (1994) *Planning Long Term Placements Study: Local Authorities Experiences in Planning and Achieving Long Term Placements for Children.*

NINTH SESSION

authorities by requiring external scrutiny of the plan for the care of the child. Parental responsibility was awarded to the local authorities in the Children Act on the basis of their legal mandate, their control over key resources to manage substitute care and the belief that the pesonnel had the necessary knowledge and skills, reinforced by an appropriate management system to track children's progress. The proposed changes would imply that this position had been wrong and, additionally, that the courts were better placed to manage long-term planning strategies.

The Children Act also sought to restrict court interventions whenever possible. Prolonging the possibility of court involvement would erode this principle. Its rationale under present law was set out clearly in the words of one of the judges interviewed in the Sussex study:

> 'I think it is debilitating for the families, both the adults and children involved, because they feel there is no finality ... because in three or six months or a year you have got to return to court and it all may be changed ... So, I think it is better to have a once and for all hearing to have the issues examined, debated and for the judge to make his or her findings and his decision and then it is over. You get out of the legal system and it is then up to those who have been entrusted with the care of the child to do their best to make the plans work.'

As this quotation makes clear, the proposed new measures could also have implications for the partnership principles in the Act between social services and families. Finally, the proposals involve an issue of justice in relation to the welfare of the child. On what basis would the powers be limited to one year? While it is easy to answer this question in terms of feasibility, it is harder to explain the logic on the ground of principle. The obligation to promote the welfare of the child does not stop after one year, even if one might wish to argue that such a period is critical and may have a disproportionate effect on later welfare outcomes.[1] Cases which would involve 'inappropriate' changes in plans or drift after the one-year limit would be forced to rely on local authority internal complaints procedures or an application by parents to discharge the order. In effect, a two-tier system of remedy would be created, which could be perceived to be unjust.

These are all points of principle. However, the central question now to be asked from a pragmatic view is whether any of the difficulties that have been identified in post-order implementation could be overcome by introducing new monitoring functions as outlined above. The specific issues are delay in implementation of the plan, drift, breakdown of placements and resource shortfalls (whether of placements or personnel or both). As a preliminary observation, the obvious point must be made that the primary legislation would need amendment since the GAL becomes *functus officio* (ie has no legal remit to monitor the case) after the order has been made and this is also the position of the courts.

Monitoring by an external body, such as the guardian ad litem, could help ensure that the planning momentum during court applications would be maintained thereafter, provided that the reasons for slippage lay within the control of the local authority. Furthermore, if a plan for reunification has run into difficulties, social services might welcome court backing for the child's removal to an out of home placement as it could potentially reduce tensions in managing a failing partnership between the local authority and parents. Local authorities used to sometimes find the powers vested in the High Court in wardship very useful in particularly difficult cases. But extending the guardian's duties would place new financial constraints on local authorities, as they would be expected to meet the guardian's costs and this would reduce the already stretched budget for children's services. There would additionally be the extra costs of time spent in preparation of court reports and attendance at court. These would impact both on social services personnel and the local authority solicitors. Similarly, there would be additional burdens on the courts, which could exacerbate the existing delays in hearing cases. There are two further important points. First, there is a risk of undermining the authority and status of social services. Secondly, given that the costs of these changes would divert already stretched resources from other children in need, this policy would require strong justification.

But some of the problems that Hunt and Macleod's study identified in post-care order implementation may not be amenable to court resolution. Some obvious examples include problems in finding a suitable adoptive placement or long-term foster carer. Nor is it easy to see how the courts could resolve problems of social work turnover, for these matters concern social services' management and funding. Complexity is another issue which may create as many difficulties for the court as for social services. Older children too pose particularly difficult management issues and their placements are more vulnerable to breakdown.

---

1 See Millham, S et al (1986) *Lost in Care: the Problems of Maintaining Links between Children in Care and their Families*, Gower.

There are some further thorny questions posed by the proposed reform strategies. First, how will a judgment be reached that 'the change in the detail of the plan is significantly contrary to the welfare of the child'? Against what yardstick will 'significance' be judged and on what basis would the court or guardian's view be preferred to that of social services? This calls into question the broader issue of the present state of our knowledge to predict children's futures reliably and what kinds of information would be needed to give preference to one set of predictions as against another. Similar issues are raised by the second threshold criterion – the judgment that the plan has become 'inappropriate' because of unforeseen circumstances. Arguably, the social services have the best knoweldge of the circumstances of the case overall and it should be possible to be confident that social services will alter course 'appropriately' if circumstances change unexpectedly.

The much larger question that underlies this call for legal reform is about confidence in the capacity of social services to effectively manage cases post care order. As argued earlier, if this is the issue, first the evidence must be compelling. If it should prove to be so, then a whole range of strategies would need consideration. A review power would certainly be included in the arsenal of possible measures, but so would the possibility of introducing accredited child care staff in the way that legislation requires approved social workers in the field of mental health. There might also be a need for better training and more effective management strategies to make the review framework work well. Hunt and Macleod, for example, suggested that the primary need was for the local authority to get its house in order on implementation and review and to take a more corporate responsibility for children on care orders. These are the long-term issues which may need to be addressed at some future point. In the short term, there are a number of measures which could be introduced immediately without any major changes of principle to existing law.

SOME PROPOSALS FOR STRENGTHENING THE CARE PLANNING SYSTEM: THE NEXT STEPS

This conference has put forward a wealth of suggestions to tackle the concerns that have been raised. Some of these are modest proposals which have the advantage of building on existing structures and could therefore be implemented quite easily. This final section to the paper will consider both measures identified at the conference and some additional suggestions.

Increasing scrutiny of the care plan in individual cases

One of the most obvious points to emerge from the conference is the need to increase the scrutiny of the plan prior to the making of the order by all those involved. More questioning at the pre-trial stage with particular attention to resources, costings, timescales and placement details is a first and obvious step. This scrutiny should also be directed to commitments made by agencies other than social services, such as housing, health and education. But at the final hearing too, it may be important to ensure greater scrutiny, particularly when there is a change of heart during proceedings, in order to test the commitment of child and family to the plan. The plan is unlikely to work without this. Special safeguards may also be necessary for parents with learning difficulties.

Where more persistent difficulties arise over the quality of care plans, the matter should be taken up by the court either with the local authority direct, or via the Family Court Business Committee. This Committee is well placed to fulfil this role, precisely because it was set up to examine processes and procedures at local level when difficulties were experienced.

Finally, the proposals to redraft the DH guidance in Volume 3 into thematic blocks may help increase clarity of thinking in care planning. Whilst this measure is to be welcomed, it would be insufficient by itself because the requirements for specificity and detail are already there. For this reason, a more general approach to resolving some of the existing tensions will be necessary as well as measures directed at individual case planning.

General measures to enhance shared expectations and to discuss difficulties

On a more general level, the local Family Court Business Committee seems the ideal forum for interdisciplinary discussions in which mutual expectations of care plans could be explored. More training on care plan formulation, and especially inter-disciplinary training, is another obvious next step to help improve the quality of care plans and enhance shared expectations. In this regard, inter-disciplinary training is especially important because this conference has highlighted some significant value debates about levels of acceptable and unacceptable risk and the remedies to address these, as well as raising important issues around boundaries to professional responsibilities.

Providing feedback to the courts and to guardians ad litem on the outcomes of their decisions

It is worth considering whether steps should be taken to increase feedback to both guardians ad litem and the courts on the outcomes of their decisions. Interestingly, in the Sussex judicial interviews, there was a mixed reaction to the suggestion of receiving regular feedback on cases. The additional burden this measure would place on social services was one reason for this, another was the view that there was little practical advantage in knowing the outcome of the case unless courts had greater post-order powers. But others thought that feedback could provide a useful learning tool and this conference has demonstrated forcefully the absence of any mechanism at present to enable the courts to learn about case outcome. It could play a particularly valuable role in the small but significant minority of cases where the order has been made by the judge in the face of grave uncertainty about the outcome. It should be possible to arrange for the Family Court Business Committee to inform both the courts and guardians ad litem from time to time about the progress of their cases and, possibly, to earmark specific cases for post order feedback. This could usefully be done at local level, but consideration should also be given to providing some system of national feedback.

Strengthening local authority reviewing procedures

A high proportion of local authorities are now using the *Looking After Children*[1] system which provide a lot of information about all aspects of the child's upbringing and will eventually shed light on the outcome of different types of placement. Part of this framework is a common review system, which involves completion of *Action and Assessment Records* which cover seven[2] key dimensions of child functioning. The assessment materials measure the individual progress of looked after children. They also contain an implementation element because practitioners are required to consider what action needs to be taken, within what time-scales and by whom to ensure the child's welfare is monitored and promoted actively. These materials should improve planning for all looked after children including those on court orders.

CONCLUSIONS

Three main questions were posed at the outset of this paper. First, was there evidence of substantive difficulty? Secondly, would a post-order review mechanism address those difficulties and what alternatives or additional strategies should be considered? The answer to the first question must be that some concerns have been identified but the jury is still out. The available evidence is far too mixed to be able to answer the question affirmatively or negatively. The existing studies have not been able to address some of the key questions on the relationship between care planning with the courts, social services implementation and child welfare outcomes. Furthermore, the evidence on the kinds of information that need to go into care plans is far from clear, so is the matter of the key determinants of outcome. Nor has it yet been possible to analyse how well social services maintain services and contact arrangements or how partnership with parents and children work in these highly charged situations. The focus has tended to be on placements and how far they endure. As the study by Sinclair and Grimshaw indicates the success of contact plans and the child's progress in health and education are all crucial dimensions for evaluating success and difficulty in care planning. Given these information deficits and the relative lack of information on the size of the problem, there seems little basis to implement any major changes at this point as the remedies might be misplaced.

---

1 See Department of Health (1995) *Looking After Children: Good Parenting, Good Outcomes – Management and Implementation Guide*, HMSO. Also see Ward, H (ed) *Looking After Children: Research into Practice, Second Report to the Department of Health on Assessing Outcomes in Child Care*, HMSO. The Working Party on Child Care Outcomes was first set up by the Department of Health in 1987.

2 The seven areas comprise health, education, identity, family and social relationships, social presentation, emotional and behavioural development and self-care skills. The Working Party on Child Care Outcomes considered that progress along these seven dimensions is necessary for the attainment of satisfactory outcomes, which were defined as 'long-term well-being in adulthood'.

This brings us to the second question on legal reform. When all the evidence is available, it may point in the direction of legal remedy. If it does, other alternatives to the present emphasis on post-order review may need consideration. One possibility was put forward in the Adoption Bill 1996, namely the proposal to make care plans mandatory. Consideration could also be given to introducing more formal requirements for certain kinds of information to be provided in the care plan. It may be argued that a universal system is less invidious than one which ferrets out failures for review.

In the meantime, the modest proposals outlined here can only improve care planning. Should these measures prove inadequate and if it were to be found that care planning was unable to achieve the objectives of legislation, a far broader review of strategy would be needed. This would include, in addition to consideration of legal reform, a major rethink of the way in which we deliver services to a group of children who are amongst the most vulnerable and difficult to help.

Acknowledgements

I am grateful to my colleague, Dr Morag Owen, for her part in the preliminary analysis of the data.

WORKING GROUP RESOLUTIONS: THE RESULTS

INTRODUCTION

The task of the Working Group Sessions was said at the outset of the conference to be to take forward the fifth conference aim:

> 'To draw out policy and practice issues which may require further attention'.

Each Working Group was asked to produce a summary of its proposals for addressing the concerns that had been raised at the conference about care plans and their implementation. The six groups' proposals and that of the mental health delegates to the conference (who produced their own separate proposal) are set out in this chapter as they were presented to the conference.

WORKING GROUP A

1 A MULTI-DISCIPLINARY MEETING of all professionals between formulation and finalisation of care plans in order to achieve agreed realistic care plan, balancing individual needs against available resources with crucial starred goals and time-scales. In the event of disagreement within the professional group the judge will decide.

2 In the event of a failure to implement any starred goal, that failure to be reported by the social services department to the GAL.

Action

(a) The GAL endeavours to understand and resolve by inter-disciplinary routes.
(b) In the event of failure, GAL to refer 'breakdown' to Director of Social Services.
(c) In the event that the GAL remains concerned, the matter to be referred to the court.

WORKING GROUP B

(1) Prior to making a care order

The care plan needs:

(a) to identify by name the senior responsible officer;
(b) to state how the plan will be implemented;
(c) to include consultation with other disciplines;
(d) to present the costings which have been agreed and their proportion of the total available annual budget for children looked after by the local authority.

The care plan will be the responsibility of the senior responsible officer referred to in (a) above who will exercise parental oversight on behalf of the local authority throughout the life of the care order.

(2) Post-care order

Courts and guardian panels to receive data from the local authority's six-monthly review of the care plan, in aggregate. In addition, courts and guardians to receive, exceptionally, copies of individual care plan reviews as identified on a case-by-case basis according to agreed criteria.

Suggestions for the agreed criteria are:

(a) if the court so directs at the time of making the order;
(b) if the time for implementing any significant aspect of the care plan has passed;
(c) the care plan has changed in a material way;
(d) the senior responsible officer wishes the court to have the care plan review.

It is recommended that the aggregate data should be collected nationally and published on an annual basis.

The information so collected and collated should be reviewed after a two-year period and a decision then taken as to whether or not any changes are required. These matters should all be considered by the Lord Chancellor's Advisory Board on Family Law.

WORKING GROUP C

(1) A good review process needs:

(a) expertise in child care;
(b) an independent element;
(c) continuing oversight;
(d) power to deliver solutions.

(2) A good local authority process could and should contain all four of the above via:

(a) a senior specialist arm's length review officer;
(b) review panels with independent members to consider problem cases.

(3) Courts are not best suited to the review process as they cannot provide all four of (1)(a)–(d) above:

(a) they arguably have (1)(a);
(b) they certainly have (1)(b);
(c) they cannot realistically have (1)(c); and
(d) certainly cannot have (1)(d).

WORKING GROUP D

(1) On making a care order the Court may attach a condition/direction as to the manner in which the local authority is to carry out its duties under the order, provided it is satisfied that:

(a) the case is exceptional; and
(b) the attachment of the condition/direction is required for the welfare of the child; and
(c) the cost of complying with the condition is reasonable and proportionate; and
(d) unless the condition/direction is attached, the aims of the condition/direction would not be achieved (ie the local authority will not agree to do it voluntarily).

(2) A local authority may at any time apply to the court for a variation or discharge of a condition/direction attached under (1) above (the machinery for an administrative review of the operation of the care order to be along the lines suggested by Tess Duncan (see Appendix to her paper) with filters before ultimate further recourse to court, probably with a requirement of leave and to be initiated within a stated time-limit, perhaps 12 months).

(3) Upon an application for review of a care order the court may exercise any of its powers on an application for a care order, including its power under (1) above.

WORKING GROUP E

Key issues:

(a) Care planning;
(b) Review process.

– 'Starred' key factors: must be implemented within specified time-scales. Failure to do so would trigger a review.

- Certificate of compliance: should be filed at court by the responsible officer. Failure to do so could be potential trigger for review.
- GAL appropriate person to intervene: as an alternative to the court process, the GAL could have *locus standi* to use the local authority complaints process with the right to complain on behalf of the child.

WORKING GROUP F

Key issues:

(1) Importance of preventive work: there should be good strategies for *all* children with targeted plans in an inter-agency context, with perhaps a designated professional in education and health who promotes interdisciplinary co-operation.

(2) Quality of the care plan: there should be only one care plan document. Care should be taken when composing the plan to ensure it:

- is individual;
- is specific;
- sets out measures; and
- gives alternatives.

(3) Effective monitoring systems: if feasible

- GAL brings back 'failed' plans;
- local authority brings back 'failed' plans;
- an independent visitor prompts a return to court, although evidence as to the problems would be needed.

CHILD AND ADOLESCENT MENTAL HEALTH DELEGATES

Proposals for addressing concerns about improving care plans and their implementation

Time 1: GAL report submitted.

Time 2: Social services produces care plan according to set protocol – aims, needs, specific plans, timetable, starred 'core' elements etc.

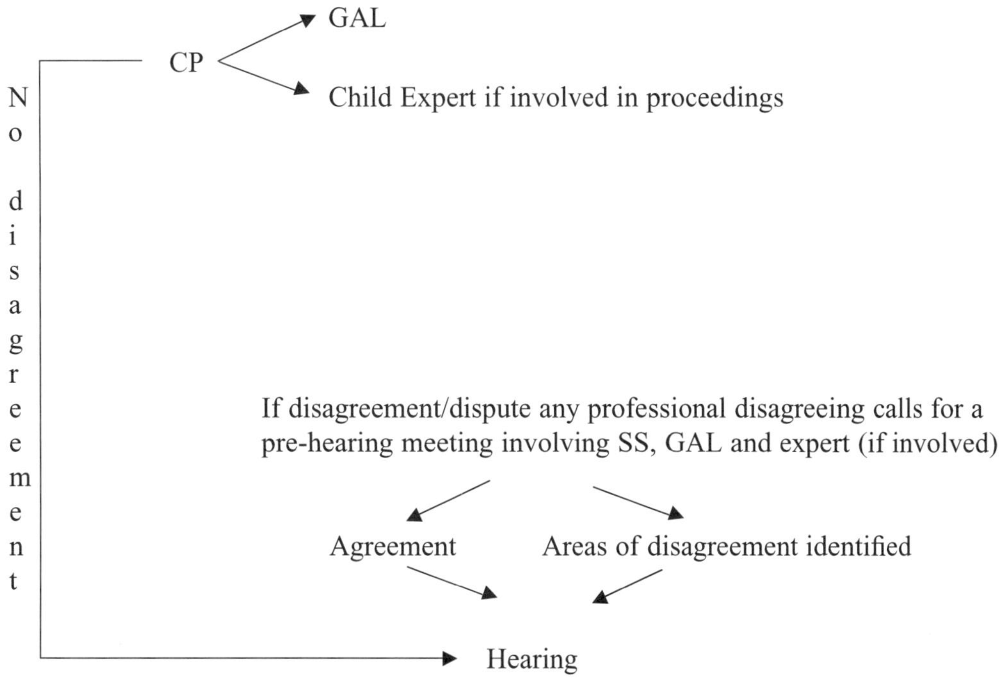

Time 3: 'Judge led', care plan as part of order.

Time 4: Development of internal social service audit/review mechanisms – 'independent' review teams.

one-year pilot: all review minutes to the GAL *or* judge involved in case

- audit of information gathered eg in how many cases are there significant changes to starred* items

CONFERENCE REVIEW: CLOSING REMARKS

The Rt Hon Lord Justice Thorpe

Lord Justice Thorpe expressed his thanks to the President's Inter-Disciplinary Committee, in particular to the sub-committee who had been involved in an immense amount of advance planning for the conference (Arran Poyser, Tess Duncan and Peter Harris in particular) and also to those who had written papers for the conference in addition to their usual professional responsibilities.

He said that the conference had brought to the fore the fundamental concept of preventative strengthening of the care process in the initial care planning stages to try and reduce the number of cases failing in their implementation. He emphasised the valuable input of the mental health professionals in this regard and noted that as specialist professionals in the field all members of the conference were empowered to change the practice in their particular field as a result of what had been discussed. Lord Justice Thorpe cited as an example of this the proposal to organise an inter-disciplinary meeting between the formulation of the care plan and its finalisation to ensure that it was as realistic and specific as could be achieved. This was something that could be immediately implemented as a point of practice, perhaps by a trial judge making a specific direction at the timetabling stage of a case.

More difficult was the question of changes to practice and/or legislative changes to the process after the making of an order, although he noted that there was something approaching a consensus that the guardian should have some continuing role after the making of a care order. The challenge for the President's Committee was to take forward the tentative conclusions reached. In that regard, he welcomed any contributions from those not members of that committee but interested in the inter-disciplinary work of the family judicial system.

CONTINUATION OF THE CONFERENCE

THE FUTURE: KEY PRACTICE ISSUES

This section has been produced by a professional sub-group comprising of Dr Claire Sturge, Consultant Child Psychiatrist; Dr Judith Trowell, Consultant Child Psychiatrist; Dr Danya Glaser, Consultant Child Psychiatrist; Mr Arran Poyser, Social Services Inspector, DoH; Tess Duncan, Surrey Panel of Guardians ad Litem and Reporting Officers; and Michael Leadbetter, Director of Social Services, Essex.

The group members were of the view that a further meeting could produce a range of options and some questions, which would help readers focus on some of the key messages from the conference.

This chapter, supplemented by an Appendix of questions produced by Peter Kemp, Director of Social Services for Durham County Council, is produced to take forward the key practice issues raised in this book.

Introduction

The final presentations by the working groups at the end of the conference clearly carried some core messages common to all. There was a shared desire to carry foward certain messages in the interests of children in the care system, and not lose the impetus of so much thought, debate and consideration given to the many relevant issues.

This paper is an attempt to encapsulate those shared visions and the common commitment to improve children's situations.

The core elements or themes shared by all the groups were:

(1) The importance of Care Plans in:

- a bringing together of views of all those involved about the needs of the child;
- the provision of a profile of needs, specific to an individual child at a particular point in time;
- monitoring for future care and planning – even in the face of changing social workers;
- a good and practical plan which is considered a best match for the needs of that child.

Participants who had begun the conference feeling that as social services had the jurisdiction to cock a snook at the options of others on their plans, including the views of judges, and that, therefore, investing too much effort into getting them right was often a waste of time, shifted to feeling that perseverance could achieve a better plan for the child which could have lifelong implications for their well-being. Cynicism became a wish for positive change.

It was, of course, recognised that Care Plans are not infallible. They may as events unfold prove misguided, or for very good reason, need to change.

(2) Children are very vulnerable within the care system and need every effort by those involved at a pivotal point in their lives to produce a plan for him or her, which can act to safeguard that child's future.

(3) The importance of inter-disciplinary working in this area. A real partnership between those involved can produce a good, balanced and realistic plan. If there are significant disagreements over the plan, then means are needed to resolve these. Different disciplines can make different contributions.

(4) Where the 'battle' for parents is over the threshold criteria and that this prevents any attention, realistic consideration or energy being invested in the Care Plan, then a threshold ('split') hearing may hold many advantages. With the threshold criteria issue resolved, parents can address the implications of this and planning can take a new direction.

(5) The infrastructure in any locality is all important. Care Plans can be meaningless unless there are systems in place for parental partnership, joint working and inter-agency co-operation. Lack of resources or lack of commitment by local services to the needs of children in care can undermine a Care Plan, however good. A culture of caring and preventative work will be the foundation on which any Care Plan is built.

(6) Audit is important. While delegates had horrific stories of drift or reversal of Care Plans after proceedings and a feeling that major problems are common, there is no information on the level of serious problems which may be set against the proportion of Care Plans where no significant problems are encountered.

Overall the message was: Cherish the Care Plan – Get it Right.

Informing Care Plans

There are considerable concerns about the perceived failure to implement Care Plans and concerns about the damage caused by delay, drift and failure to proide what is recommended for the child.

> **Suggestion 1:** Large sums of money are spent on investigations, expert assessment and lengthy court proceedings. In some cases the parties should be informed that this is the budget allocations for the child, it can be spent on arguing the case or on providing services, help, support, therapy for the child, the carers, and the family. Perhaps, some families would then settle using family group conferences, specialist child care mediation, or some form of conciliation, arbitration or mediation.

The Care Plan is generally based on a great deal of assessment work and may be written using the expert report, or may not.

> **Suggestion 2:** Involve experts in drawing up the care plan, use their knowledge and experience both general and for this particular case.

Care Plans once written and agreed in court and orders given, can appear to be set aside. Care Plans need to be implemented. 'Cherish the Care Plan' consists of valuing it as an agreed way forward for the child that needs implementing as soon as possible. Resource issues need to have been realistically considered whilst drawing up the Care Plan.

The threshold stage

A Care Plan is only required following the fulfilment of the threshold criteria. However, the content of the Care Plan is partly dependent on the parents' acceptance of, and response to, a finding of significant harm. If this is being disputed up to the point of the final hearing, it is often unreasonable to predict the parents' subsequent response if a finding of significant harm is made. In these situations, the Care Plan would need to address the alternative possibilities that the parents would either recognise the significant harm, and their predicted response to this or that the parent would be unable to accept the court's findings.

> **Suggestion 3:** Where there is a dispute over the threshold criteria it is preferable to make a finding at an earlier hearing, thus utilising the time between that hearing and the final hearing to accommodate the parents' response in the Care Plan.

Shaping the Care Plan

Social Workers and their agents eg NSPCC, guardian ad litem and experts (when appointed) will all have carried out their coordinated, though independent, assessments in preparation for the final hearing. The Care Plan is drawn up and re-designed by social services in the light of others' assessments as well as social services own plans. Not infrequently, various professional contributors have some differences of opinion regarding the Care Plan to be presented to court. It is therefore useful for social services, the guardian and the expert (if instructed) to meet prior to the final hearing and after completion of prospective assessments, in order to reach consensus on the details of the plan. It is also useful at that meeting to 'star' those aspects of the care plan whose fulfilment is of primary importance for the child's subsequent well-being and whose fulfilment would therefore require particular monitoring at specified times following the eventuality of an order being granted.

> **Suggestion 4:** A meeting should be held with all the parties, along the lines of the experts' meeting, with an understanding that the professionals will endeavour genuinely to try and see the issues from the others' viewpoint. This will allow a fuller and freer airing of the issues, which the formalities of court do not allow. Each party should produce a skeleton argument to clarify their position, and circulate it before the meeting. This will allow a focus on areas of agreement and disagreement, and assist the meeting to be used efficiently.

Certain principles need to be adopted by the professionals to ensure a process which keeps the child's welfare at the forefront. These include a belief that confrontation and a desire to 'win' are not conducive to good practice. A model for professional behaviour is the protocol between the guardian and the social worker. This states at the beginning of a case how areas of disagreement may be resolved and enables communication which assists in establishing a calm and professional approach and a dialogue focused on the welfare of the child. Any undercurrents, such as 'I know better than you' which may be affecting behaviour, must be avoided.

> **Suggestion 5:** At the meeting suggested in Suggestion 4 the participants shoud seek consensus as far as possible and identify with the greatest possible clarity any differences which remain and the reasons for those differences. This should be in the form of a supplementary report to assist the judge.

Ideally, any differences which are aired in court should arise either from the evidence itself or from the parties' differing analyses which require the court's adjudication. While these may refer to the threshold criteria, they can also focus on child welfare and the details of the Care Plan. It is regrettable if professional differences of opinion about child welfare are left to court arbitration for want of pre-court dialogue and discussion.

The management of reviews

It is largely accepted that the reviewing and monitoring of Care Plans (and indeed other linked matters, for example child protection registration and planning) are best undertaken with a degree of independence. However, total separation of responsibility for reviewing and monitoring from day-to-day operation of services, leads to the well-documented problems posed by the separation of power and responsibility.

Many authorities grappling with these potentially inherent conflicts have come up with a variety of mechanisms for ensuring an appropriate degree of impartiality whilst maintaining appropriate responsibility within the management structure of the social services department.

Examples include:

- (a) Independent Chairs, perhaps as part of a group of independent Chairs or through arrangements with a voluntary organisation.
- (b) Reviews undertaken by a manager from a different specialism or section of the department.
- (c) A review and monitoring section within the department, but reporting directly to the Head of Child Care or a senior manager.

Other proposals arising from the workshop included:

- (a) Giving responsibility for monitoring and reviewing Care Plans to the guardian ad litem for perhaps six to 12 months following their agreement by the court.
- (b) Giving judges the power to review Care Plans in particular circumstances.

> **Suggestion 6:** On balance we would argue that authorities, who do not have an arm's length reviewing team in their structure, should give serious consideration to setting up independent units answerable to the senior child care manager within the department. This gives, in our view, the appropriate degree of independence, but keeps responsibility and authority within the department, and in most hierarchies only one removed from the Director. Hence, the Director and the Head of Child Care can be held accountable through the proper democratic mechanisms for the conduct of their staff in relation to Care Planning.

These arrangements can also be instrumental in monitoring the quality of services, aggregating information through reviews of looked after children, and introducing new practice developments.

In the Appendix to this chapter are a series of questions which could be used by social service departments in bench-marking good practice.

Feedback

Other agencies, health, education and the legal domain – both judges and guardians ad litem, feel frustrated and powerless as they see Care Plans ignored and children left. They do not hear about the successes. They only hear about the problems and failures when a case has unexpectedly changed and the Care Plan is inappropriate and needs to be revised. There is an opportunity when a case is reviewed for the summary to provide valuable feedback to the professionals involved, in order to inform their recommendations.

Suggestion 7: The ADSS (Association of Directors of Social Services) could set in place a system where at case reviews a summary goes to the relevant judge, GAL, expert and DoH named individual. The summaries could be collated also by each local authority, judge, GAL and expert. In this way local authorities, judges, GALs and experts can review and learn from their practice. If all the local authorities brought their data on follow-up together an overall picture could be available across England and Wales.

Social services departments face particular criticism because it is they who must implement the decisions in the Care Plan. There is a risk that they will respond to criticism in a defensive manner. We must recognise that we all make mistakes and get things wrong and that all the participants in devising the Care Plan have a role to play in assisting social services departments when mistakes have been made. This should assist them to acknowledge this and use it as a learning process.

Suggestion 8: Where cases have gone wrong or the Care Plan has been ignored social services departments should inform previously involved professionals and seek help.

Audit of implementation of Care Plans

As well as a system of feedback for the professionals involved, concerns are such that a systematic review is needed to clarify the extent of the problem. There are a number of different ways to carry this out.

A prospective audit could follow cases coming before certain High Court and county court judges over a three-month period and their progress then monitored for, say, two years. If this were to be adopted, care would need to be taken to ensure that results were not skewed by the professionals' awareness of the monitoring.

A retrospective audit could look at cases either appearing before certain judges in the High Court and county court, say between January and March 1997; or the court cases from certain local authorities between January and March 1996. Care would need to be taken to ensure a representative sample. We could see what the outcome has been and what became of the Care Plan.

Another possibility would be to review retrospectively all the cases coming to, say, the High Court in London (Family Division) over a period and follow them up. This would, of course, only study the more complex cases.

Suggestion 9: A review of cases, their outcomes and how the Care Plan was implemented should be set up. Funding will need to be sought for a researcher, consultation and supervision could be provided by a sub-group of the Interdisciplinary Committee. It might be a suitable project for a senior psychiatric registrar.

Conclusion

Social workers and social services departments feel themselves to be under siege, constantly attacked, their work denigrated. It is vitally important that their role and tasks are valued and their position in society strengthened, so that they are seen as a respected profession. Social workers who write and implement care plans need to have received a thorough training, preferably three years post graduate. There needs to be a Social Work Council equivalent to the disciplinary bodies for other professions, such as, the General Medical Council for doctors, so that bad social workers are dealt with in a professional way. There needs to be recognition that social workers are involved in rationing in the same way as the health service and this involves painful and difficult decisions. We all, and the legal domain particularly, focus on a particular child, a particular family, but we are also members of our society and know there are budgetary restraints which mean there must be a balance, the claims come from many sides. Many children are in need, or in need of protection. The resources are limited, the demands infinite.

APPENDIX

Key questions

Arising out of this paper are some key questions which we need to consider to take account of the views (and prejudices) about the role and performance of social services departments expressed at the conference.

1. Should the oversight of the implementation of the Care Plan rest solely with the team manager; is the role of the child care coordinator in case reviews sufficient to safeguard the integrity of the Care Plan?
2. A number of judges expressed a view that social workers often felt intimidated, devalued and de-skilled during the court process. Is there evidence of this in your department and, if so, what can be done to support social workers in court and strengthen the significance of their evidence?
3. Given the length of time that care proceedings can take, are we doing sufficient to guard against case 'drift' and how can this be monitored?
4. Can we begin to produce costed Care Plans so that we can test cost-effectiveness and assess the impact of Care Planning decisions on local budgets?
5. Are there specific services that are unavailable which cause us to compromise when drawing up Care Plans, eg mental health services for children; post-abuse trauma services; adoption and fostering placements. If so, can we project those needs into our forward planning cycle in order to achieve their delivery at the appropriate time?
6. Do we need to adapt our concept of adoption in light of the increasing number of cases in which adopted children are seeking out their birth parents?
7. Are we experiencing delays in:
   - care proceedings, eg securing appropriate assessments and expert advice;
   - implementing Care Plans due to lack of resources;
   - in deciding that the Care Plan is not working and then changing the elements?
8. Where rehabilitation with the natural family is the focus of a Care Plan are we clear enough about the key indicators for success and the time-scales within which rehabilitation will be attempted?
9. Can we improve our assessment processes in families so that we can develop clearer and more focused intervention strategies, thus building up our preventive services?
10. Can we develop performance indicators based on Assessing Outcomes materials which might help us to define Care Plan success or the success of a placement, eg school attendance; number of placements; contact rate with family?
11. Are we consciously gathering evidence from research findings to inform our practice and to develop evidence-based intervention?
12. Do we need to develop our assessment of the potential of extended families to care for children, eg use of family group for conferencing?
13. Can we achieve regular, aggregated feedback from the GALRO Panel on social work practice in the department?
14. Do we need to develop protocols between the GAL and social worker that will avoid misunderstandings, delays and disruption in the process of taking care proceedings?
15. A Yorkshire pilot scheme is looking at the value of a meeting between the GAL, social worker and the team manager early in the care proceedings process to identify difficulties and obstacles in the process in an attempt to speed up decision making. Would this type of meeting be useful in the context of our services?

APPENDIX I

CONFERENCE AIMS

- To explore key issues facing local authorities in planning children's services and in preparing care plans for court proceedings
- To ascertain how best care planning processes involve all appropriate disciplines relevant to the child's needs
- To assess the use of care plans in court setting
- To consider how care plans are subsequently implemented, reviewed and amended; and the outcomes for children in local authority care
- To draw out policy and practice issues which may require further attention
- To publish a report of the conference proceedings

PROGRAMME

Sunday 14 September

16.30–17.30	*Arrival, Registration, Tea*
17.30–17.45	WELCOMING ADDRESS Sir Stephen Brown *The President of the Family Division*
17.45–18.10	PLENARY 1 Chair: Lord Justice Thorpe A JUDICIAL PERSPECTIVE OF CARE PLANS Mr Justice Wall
18.10–18.45	DISCUSSION
19.30	*Dinner*

NOTE: Workshop Groups
Each Conference Member has been allocated to a Workshop Group. The first named member of each group is asked to chair the Group for the first session on Monday at least.

Monday 15 September

09.00–09.30	PLENARY 2 Chair: Sir Stephen Brown MEDICAL INPUT TO CARE PLANNING Dr Clare Sturge *Northwick Park Hospital* Jenny Kenrick *Tavistock Clinic*
09.35–10.30	WORKING GROUPS Session 1
10.30–11.00	*Coffee*
11.00–11.30	PLENARY 3 Chair: Sir Stephen Brown LOCAL AUTHORITIES AND CARE PLANNING – PAPER 1 Peter Kemp *Director of Social Services, Durham* Steven Ford *Social Services Department, Durham*
11.35–12.30	WORKING GROUPS Session 2
12.30–14.00	*Lunch*

14.00–14.30	PLENARY 4
	Chair: Sir Stephen Brown
	RESEARCH MESSAGES RELEVANT TO CARE PLANNING
	Professor Olive Stevenson
14.30–15.00	DISCUSSION
	MARKET PLACE (*see note at end*)
15.00–15.30	Poster feedback display from Working Groups Sessions 1 and 2
15.30–16.00	*Tea*
16.00–16.30	PLENARY 5
	CARE PLANNING – A DEPARTMENT OF HEALTH STUDY
	Arran Poyser *Social Services Inspectorate*
16.35–17.30	WORKING GROUPS Session 3
17.35–18.10	PLENARY 6
	Chair: Sir Stephen Brown
	OVERVIEW AND IMPRESSIONS – KEY ISSUES ARISING FROM DAY 2
	Michael Leadbetter *Director of Social Services, Essex*
19.30	*Dinner*

Tuesday 16 September

09.00–09.30	PLENARY 7
	Chair: Peter Harris
	GUARDIANS AND CARE PLANS
	Tess Duncan *Panel Manager, Surrey*
09.35–10.30	WORKING GROUPS Session 4
10.30–11.00	*Coffee*
11.00–11.30	PLENARY 8
	Chair: Dr Hamish Cameron
	LOCAL AUTHORITIES AND CARE PLANNING – PAPER 2
	Anne Chan *Assistant Director of Social Services, Southwark*
	Gloria McFarlane *Social Services Department, Southwark*
11.35–12.30	WORKING GROUPS Session 5
12.30–14.00	*Lunch*
	MARKET PLACE (*see note at end*)
14.00–14.40	Poster feedback from Working Groups Sessions 3, 4 and 5
14.45–15.15	FINAL PLENARY 9
	Chair: Lord Justice Thorpe
	OBSERVATIONS
	Professor Judith Harwin *University of Sussex*
15.15–15.30	CLOSING REMARKS
	Lord Justice Thorpe
15.30	*Tea and Depart*

NOTE – Market Place following Working Group Sessions

The task of each Working Group Session is to take forward the fifth conference aim:

'To draw out policy and practice issues which may require further attention'

- Attention should be also given to *how* these issues might be addressed and *who* might be involved.
- Each Working Group Session should have as its product at least one flip chart sheet of (legible!) key issues. These sheets will be displayed in the main Plenary Room at each of the two Market Places.
- The flip charts should be displayed for the Market Place feedback (Monday 15.00–15.30; Tuesday 14.00–14.40).
- Each Working Group should ensure that one or two of their members are positioned alongside their group's flip charts. They should be able to explain to other conference delegates the group's thinking and how they envisage the policy or practice issues might be taken forward/implemented in the future.

APPENDIX II

LIST OF PARTICIPANTS

His Honour Judge Martin Allweis
His Honour Judge Christopher Barnett QC
Professor Michael Berger *Chair of Psychology, Royal Holloway & Bedford College*
Susan Bindman
The Honourable Mrs Justice Joyanne Bracewell
The Rt Hon Sir Stephen Brown *President of the Family Division*
His Honour Judge David Brunning
Kathy Butcher
Deborah Cameron *Director of Social Services, London Borough of Newham*
Dr Hamish Cameron *Consultant Child Psychiatrist*
The Honourable Mr Justice Cazalet
Anne Chan *Assistant Director, Southwark Social Services*
Elizabeth Clarke
Judith Collier
His Honour Judge Michael Cook
Sue Cooper
Dr Jonathan Dare *Consultant Child Psychiatrist, Belgrave Department of Child & Family Psychiatry*
His Honour Judge Peter De Mille
Tess Duncan *Surrey GALRO Panel*
His Honour Judge Brian A Farrer
Steven Ford *Social Worker, Durham County Council Social Services*
Dr Danya Glaser *Consultant Child Psychiatrist, Great Ormond Street Children's Hospital*
His Honour Judge Goldsack QC
Eva Gregory
The Honourable Mrs Justice Brenda Hale
His Honour Judge Victor Hall
His Honour Judge Donald Hamilton
Iain Hamilton *Jones Maidment Wilson*
Peter Harris *The Official Solicitor*
Professor Judith Harwin *University of Sussex*
Nicholas Hashagen
Julia Hennessy *Essex County Council, Social Services Department*
The Honourable Mr Justice James Holman
Rupert Hughes
His Honour Judge Richard Hutchinson
His Honour Judge Michael Hyam
Richard Jack
Dr Brian Jacobs *Consultant Child Psychiatrist, Maudsley Hospital*
Dr David Jones *Consultant Child Psychiatrist, The Park Hospital for Children*
His Honour Judge Hugh Jones
Peter Kemp *Director of Social Services, Durham County Council*
Jenny Kenrick *Child Psychotherapist, Tavistock Institute*
Michael Leadbetter *Director of Social Services, Essex County Council*
Bernadette Manning *Social Services Department, London Borough of Newham*
Gloria McFarlane *Legal Services, London Borough of Southwark*
His Honour Judge Glyn Morgan
Professor Rory Nicol *President, Royal College of Psychiatry*
Her Honour Judge Valerie Pearlman
Jill Pedley *Leicestershire County Council, Social Services Department*

Arran Poyser *Social Services Inspectorate, Department of Health*
Her Honour Judge Audrey Sander
His Honour Judge John Shand
Professor Olive Stevenson
Dr Clare Sturge *Consultant Child Psychiatrist, Northwick Park Hospital*
The Rt Hon Lord Justice Swinton-Thomas
The Rt Hon Lord Justice Matthew Thorpe
Dr Judith Trowell *Consultant Child Psychiatrist, Tavistock Institute*
The Honourable Mr Justice Nicholas Wall
Janice Welch
The Honourable Mr Justice Wilson
Dr Anne Zachary *Consultant Psychiatrist, The Portman Clinic*

APPENDIX III

MEMBERS OF THE PRESIDENT'S INTER-DISCIPLINARY COMMITTEE

Chair

The Rt Hon Lord Justice Thorpe	Royal Courts of Justice, Strand, London WC2A 2LL

Secretary

Michael Tester	Secretariat Manager, Principal Registry of the Family Division, First Avenue House, 42–49 High Holborn, London WC1V 6NP Tel: 0171 936 6976, Fax: 0171 936 6709

Members

Ann Gross	Department of Health, Wellington House, 133–155 Waterloo Road, London SE1 8UG
Arran Poyser	Social Services Inspector, Department of Health, Wellington House, 133–155 Waterloo Road, London SE1 8UG
Dr Anne Zachary	Portman Clinic, 8 Fitzjohns Avenue, London NW3 5NA
Dr Judith Trowell	The Tavistock Clinic, 120 Belsize Lane, London NW3 5BA
Deborah Cameron	Director of Social Services, Newham Council Social Services Department, 99 The Grove, Stratford, London E15 1HR
Michael Leadbetter	Director of Social Services, Essex County Council Social Services Department, PO Box 297 County Hall, Chelmsford CM1 1YS
Gillian Schofield	Lecturer in Social Work and GAL, University of East Anglia, Norwich NR4 7TJ
Tess Duncan	Panel Manager, Surrey GALRO Panel, PO Box 52, Guildford, Surrey GU4 7WL
Dr Claire Sturge	Department of Child and Adolescent Psychiatry, Northwick Park Hospital, Watford Road, Harrow, Middlesex HA1 3UJ

Dr Marion Myles	The Medical Centre, 7e Woodfield Road, London W9 3XT
Jenny Stevenson	British Psychological Society, 7 Chard Road, Edgbaston, Birmingham B15 3EN
Dr Brian Jacobs	8 Maberley Road, Upper Norwood, London SE19 2JB
The Rt Hon Lady Justice Butler-Sloss	Royal Courts of Justice
Florence Baron QC	Queen Elizabeth Building, Temple, London EC4Y 9BS
Elizabeth Clarke	Queen Elizabeth Building, Temple, London EC4Y 9BS
District Judge Angel	The Senior District Judge, PRFD, First Avenue House
The Hon Mr Justice Wall	Royal Courts of Justice
The Hon Mr Justice Kirkwood	Royal Courts of Justice
Peter Harris	The Official Solicitor, 81 Chancery Lane, London WC2A 1DD
Iain Hamilton	Jones Maidment Wilson, 5 Byrom Street, Manchester M3 4PF
Professor Mervyn Murch	Cardiff Law School, PO Box 427, Law Building, Museum Avenue, Cardiff CF1 1XD
Her Honour Judge Pearlman	c/o Michael Tester Secretariat, PRFD, First Avenue House, 42–49 High Holborn, London WC1V 6NP
Peter Sampson	The Chief Probation Officer, Gwent Probation Service, Cwmbran House, Mamhilad Park Estate, Pontypool, Gwent NP4 0XD
Trudy Klauber	The Tavistock & Portman NHS Trust, Child & Family Department, Tavistock Clinic, 120 Belsize Lane, London NW3 5BA

Jenny Kenrick	The Tavistock & Portman NHS Trust, Child & Family Department, Tavistock Clinic, 120 Belsize Lane, London NW3 5BA
A J P Butler	Chief Constable, Gloucestershire Constabulary, Police Headquarters, Holland House, Lansdown Road, Cheltenham GL51 6QH
Dr Danya Glaiser	Department of Psychological Medicine, The Hospital for Sick Children, Great Ormond Street, London WC1N 3JH
N Crichton	Metropolitan Stipendiary Magistrate, Inner London and City Family Proceedings Court, 59–65 Wells Street, London W1A 3AE
William Arnold	Family Policy Division, Lord Chancellor's Department, Selborne House, 54–60 Victoria Street, London SW1E 6QW
James Lawson	The Chief Executive, NCFP, Centre for Socio-Legal Studies, University of Bristol, Rodney Lodge, Grange Road, Clifton, Bristol BS8 4EA
Susan Bindman	NAGALRO, 56 Halford Road, Richmond, Surrey TW10 6AP